AVI

C000271802

HIGI
WRECKS & RELICS

Fourth Edition

David J Smith

Midland Publishing Limited

CONTENTS

© 1997 David J Smith
ISBN 1 85780 070 2

Published by
Midland Publishing Limited
24 The Hollow, Earl Shilton
Leicester, LE9 7NA, England
Tel 01455 847 815 Fax: 01455 841 805
E-mail: midlandbooks@compuserve.com

All rights reserved. No part of this
publication may be reproduced, stored in a
retrieval system, transmitted in any form or
by any means, electronic, mechanical or
photo-copied, recorded or otherwise,
without the written permission of the
publishers.

Design concept and layout
© Midland Publishing Limited and
Stephen Thompson Associates

Edited by Tim Crowe and Ken Ellis

Printed in England by
MN Productions, Brackmills,
Northampton, Northants.

Title Page Illustration:
The remains of BOAC DH Mosquito G-AGGF
at Glen Esk, Central Scotland.

INTRODUCTION

The present work is the culmination of 30 years of research, not forgetting the expenditure of much sweat, foot slogging and boot leather. I do not claim it to be definitive but know that it adds considerably to the information contained in the previous three editions published in 1976, 1977 and 1988 (under the title *High Ground Wrecks*) respectively and now out-of-print. A number of post-war crash sites have been included, some of the more recent ones hardly qualifying as historic but are listed as they are sometimes confusingly close to wrecks of an earlier era.

Since *High Ground Wrecks* was first published as a title in its own right in 1976, there has been little change in the 'art' of fell and hill walking. It is interesting to note that with this edition, some followers of the subject are now checking their position – and those of the wrecks they seek – with hand-held global positioning systems (GPS)!

I first wrote on the subject of high ground wrecks under that title in the 3rd edition of *Wrecks & Relics*, published in 1968. From this edition the opportunity has been taken to acknowledge that 'kick start' to the subject and that both titles are part of the Midland Publishing list, by renaming this work *High Ground Wrecks & Relics*.

My personal opinion is that the wreckage should be left undisturbed but unfortunately this view is not shared by everyone and a lot of pillaging has taken place. Recovering parts for museums is pardonable, but taking bits away to moulder in garden sheds and garages and eventually to be discarded is totally pointless. It should be remembered also that legally the wreckage of RAF and former enemy aircraft is Crown Property, and that Ministry of Defence permission is required for its removal. Responsibility for the remains of American aircraft has also been delegated to MoD.

Regrettably, in certain parts of the country – Snowdonia and the Lake District are two examples – the National Park Authorities have seen fit to organise the removal of much of the surviving wreckage. The aim, no doubt, is to eliminate an 'eyesore' but, since the pieces are all but invisible from more than a hundred yards away it seems to me to be an over-reaction. There are far worse excesses in the National Parks and I believe that these fragments on hillsides should be acknowledged as a form of memorial to the airmen who so often died in the accidents. Objectors should reflect that this tragic loss of life was part of a struggle to retain our freedom, one of whose privileges is to walk the hills. In complete contrast, the Brecon Beacons National Park actively promotes its wreck sites in a small publication.

Finally, a word of warning; the potential hazards of hill-walking are many. Beginners are urged to consult one of the numerous outdoor guides for information and advice on essential equipment and tactics. That said, there are many other aesthetic pleasures to be found in the mountains; apart from looking at the remains of old aeroplanes. Some of the wildest and most beautiful country in the British Isles is to be savoured.

I hope that readers will derive as much enjoyment from this blend of climbing, walking and aviation history as the writer.

David J Smith
Bebington, Wirral
June 1997

NOTES ON USING THIS BOOK

This book is basically organised as a series of commentaries and listings of high ground wrecks in sections covering the British Isles. roughly from north to south. The boundaries are somewhat arbitrary and, remain unchanged from the previous editions. The lists are sub-divided under aircraft type with entries listed chronologically under each type.

The map references quoted refer to the Ordnance Survey 1:50 000 Metric Map, the sheet number or, in the case of the separate Northern Ireland series, the grid letter, appearing before the six figure map reference. A simple explanation of how to plot these grid references appears in the margin of each map and the reader is reminded that the pre-metric one inch to the mile maps, dating back to the 1950s, conform to the same grid, although the sheet numbers are different.

Where the exact position of a crash site is not known, the north and south grid lines nearest to the officially recorded location are given, for example 109/66-15-. Occasionally, I have not been able to trace the geographical name, although it may appear on larger scale OS maps. In these cases, a question mark has been inserted after the appropriate sheet number.

The locations given in official records are often vague or mis-spelt, particularly where Welsh and Gaelic names are involved! Sometimes, a bearing and distance from a particular point are given or a latitude and longitude or a reference from an obsolete wartime map grid. The Operations Record Books (ORBs) of the unit to which the aircraft belonged and those of the various organisations handling or reporting the crash often give widely-differing positions for the site.

For example, according to their respective unit ORBs and the Accident Record Cards held at the MoD's Air Historical Branch, Wellingtons DV800 and HE466 *both* crashed on Snowdon. The actual positions are in the Carnedd Range, anything up to ten miles from Snowdon itself, which serves to illustrate how nebulous the supposedly authoritative sources can be.

To avoid tedious repetition, I have devised a formula to describe the extent of remaining wreckage, as last recorded.

S Small pieces

M Medium remains, eg engine(s), undercarriage, fairly large pieces of airframe.

L Large remains – alas, a rare category – where the aircraft, or at least large sections of it are reasonably intact.

X Not known, ie not visited by me or friends and correspondents.

Aircraft serial numbers with quotation marks indicate mistakes in the official records which I have not yet been able to correct. Squadron or unit codes are appended to the serial where known. Included are the names of the airfields from which the aircraft were operating and their destinations. When only one airfield is shown, it may be assumed that the subject was on a cross country navigational exercise (Navex), returning to its point of departure. Where training units possessed a satellite aerodrome, it is not always possible to determine from the ORB whether the aircraft had taken off from this or the parent station. Particularly where bomber Operational Training Units (OTUs) are concerned, there may be the occasional anomaly.

Many of the airfields in the lists are long disused, but there are a number of guides to their history and location, Patrick Stephens' *Action Stations* series being the best known.

For those readers who may not be familiar with the complicated system of RAF training and support units during the Second World War, a brief summary is as follows:

Elementary Flying Training Schools – EFTS – basic pilot training, usually on Tiger Moths or Magisters.

(Pilot) Advanced Flying Units – PAFU – conversion on Oxfords for future bomber and coastal pilots, Masters or Harvards for fighter pilots.

Operational Training Units – OTU – intensive practice in operational flying techniques and, at the same time, conversion onto heavier types of aircraft. In the case of fighter pilots, conversion onto high performance aircraft such as the Spitfire, Hurricane and Typhoon.

(Heavy) Conversion Units – HCU – for four-engined bomber crews immediately prior to joining a squadron.

Air Observer Navigation Schools, AONS – **Air Observers Schools** AOS – and **(Observers) Advanced Flying Units –** OAFU – turned out navigators, or observers as they were originally called, and bomb aimers. The designation of these schools changed as the war progressed. There were many other less important units whose names adequately describe their tasks.

The Air Transport Auxiliary was a civilian organisation whose men and women ferried aircraft for the RAF. Their regulations forbade cloud flying but, such was the importance of the job, many perished in bad weather crashes when delivering aircraft to the squadrons from Maintenance Units (MUs) or the manufacturers.

THANKS

Over the years many people have supplied information and photographs which have been valuable in the compilation of this book. Among the major contributors have been Paul and Tom Allonby, George Anderson, Barry Blunt, Roy Bonser, Mike Brennan, Stephen Burns, John Caie, Bill and Ian Carter, Victor Caruth, Neville B Cave, I A Clark, Ron Collier, Paul Connatty, Ernie Cromie, Geoff Cruikshank, Alan Curry, Hywel Davies, Dr M F Diprose, Peter Dobson, Eddie Doylerush, J Drake, Peter Durham, James Eagles, David W Earl, J D Earnshaw, Arthur Evans, Jim Ferguson, John Finch-Davies, Roger Freeman, Miss I Gordon, John Grech, Ken Haddleton, David Hanson, Richard C Harley, Philippa Hodgkiss, A Robin Hood, John Huggon, Russell Ives, Philip Jones, Gregor Lamb, R Leighton, S Leslie, Stephen Lewis, Andy Mackay, Alan Mark, Angus Martin, John Martindale, John McDonald, E McManus, Peter Moran, John Molyneux, Mick Muttit, Ronald C Niven, John Quinn, C D Radford, Alistair Robb, Harold Roberts, Nick Roberts, Michael Robson, Peter Rushden, Jim Rutland, Wallace Shackleton, Philip Shaw, Elliott Smock, David Stansfield, Ed Stephenson, B Stevens, Charles A Stewart, David Stirling, Ray Sturtivant, David E Thompson, A C Watson, David Wilson and Ralph Wood. I hope that anyone inadvertently omitted will forgive me; everyone's help, no matter how small, is appreciated, and will equally be so for future editions.

Photographs are by the author unless otherwise credited. We are sorry if some are not works of art, but please remember that some are old, and all have been taken on rare visits to often inaccessible sites, and often not under the best of conditions.

Chapter One

NORTHERN SCOTLAND

For the purposes of this book, I have defined this region as the landmass north of a line running east-west roughly through Inverness. It includes the North West Highlands, the largest wilderness in Britain and the remote mountains and moors of Sutherland. It must be emphasised that wreck-hunting trips in this area must be planned with extreme care, and proper equipment is essential.

There are surprisingly large tracts of country in which no wrecks are reported and one wonders if there are any which remain undiscovered. Certainly, if any missing aircraft still exist in Britain this is where they are likely to be found. A promising rumour involved a Focke-Wulf Condor on Mullach Coire Mhic Fhearchair in Wester Ross, but this is now known to be false. Another favourite is a Sopwith Camel allegedly found during the search for the Anson on Ben More Assynt. Again, it seems to have no foundation.

The terrain in the north was highly unsuitable for airfields, the handful established during the war meeting the minimum strategic requirements. They were the Coastal Command station at Wick and its nearby satellite at Skitten, a fighter base at Castletown, near Thurso, for their protection and also that of the Fleet Anchorage at Scapa Flow. Farther south, there was a small clutch of aerodromes along the Cromarty Firth, consisting of Tain, a large Coastal Command base, Evanton, an air gunnery school later taken over by the Fleet Air Arm, and Fearn, another Royal Naval Air Station used for training. RAF Alness, formerly Invergordon, was an important flying-boat base, relegated later in the

war to Sunderland and Catalina operational training.

Today's Inverness Airport at Dalcross was used at various times as an air gunners' school and for advanced pilot training. To the east lie the important airfields of Kinloss and Lossiemouth. They are still very much a part of the front-line RAF but in the Second World War they had a training role. Kinloss was a night bomber Operational Training Unit, No.19, equipped with Whitleys, while No.20 OTU was performing the same task at Lossiemouth with Wellingtons. Many of the aircraft were tired veterans withdrawn from the squadrons and the combination of treacherous weather, rugged mountains and inexperience proved fatal for many of the pupil crews on cross-country navigational exercises.

A particularly interesting site can be found near Berriedale, where the Sunderland III carrying the Duke of Kent and his entourage to Iceland crashed. The circumstances have long remained a mystery. A full account, together with possible answers, can be found in my article in *After the Battle* magazine No.37. The salvage team was given special orders to clear the wreckage completely, but a few fragments remain close to the Celtic Cross which commemorates the incident.

Whitley I P5005 on Burgie Hill is the famous 'DY-N' on which, during its earlier service with No.102 Squadron, the then Pilot Officer Leonard Cheshire gained the DSO. He flew the bomber back from Cologne with an enormous hole in the fuselage after flak ignited the flares. Another Whitley I, this time in Glen Carron, was returning to Yorkshire from a raid over Germany but such was the dearth of navigational aids during the early years of the war that the crew became completely lost and perished in the ensuing crash.

On the opposite side of the glen, a B-26C Marauder crew were killed when they apparently descended too soon on a ferry flight to Prestwick via Iceland. Another disaster befell the 15 occupants of a B-24H Liberator near Gairloch, all the more tragic because they were on their way home. A memorial plaque has been placed at the site.

I have included a further American aircraft, the US Navy SB2U-2 Vindicator, for interest only. Having visited it, I can confirm that only scraps of metal and blue-painted fabric are left.

The crew of the Anson I on Ben More Assynt were the only airmen apart from the Defiant pilot on Hunt Law, in Scotland, buried on high ground in Britain, the cairn of stones marking the grave having been renovated in 1985. The crash happened in the days before a proper mountain rescue service existed and it became policy thereafter to recover bodies no matter how difficult or unpleasant this might be. The Commonwealth War Graves Commission have placed a memorial beside the gateway to Inchnadamph Church listing the names of the crew.

Below: **Poignant memorial to the airmen lost on Anson N9857 on Ben More Assynt. The turret and simple cross provide a stark contrast with the cairn.**

AIRSPEED OXFORD

17.04.40	N4735	14 SFTS	Cairn Uish. Kinloss. Believed cleared.	29/187503	S
06.12.51	V3910/76	8 AFTS	Findhorn. Local flying from Dalcross.	27/903388	S

ARMSTRONG WHITWORTH WHITLEY

24.09.40	P5006	19 OTU	Ben Aigan. Navex from Kinloss, dived out of cloud.	27/31-48-	X
27.02.41	P4996	78 Sqn	Glen Carron. Lost returning to Dishforth from ops.	25/084487	S
01.05.41	P5070	612 Sqn	Scaraben. Anti-sub patrol from Wick.	17/083275	S
15.06.42	P5005	19 OTU	Burgie Hill. Turning error on controlled descent through cloud to Kinloss.	27/10-55-	X
12/13.3.42	BD678/ WL-R	612 Sqn	Ben Hutig. On convoy escort from Wick.	10/543665	S
17.05.43	BD295/M	19 OTU	Cawdor Moor. Navex from Kinloss.	27/811409	S
28.08.43	Z9469	19 OTU	Four miles south of Kinloss. Navex from Kinloss.	27/?	X

AVRO ANSON

13.04.41	N9857	19 OTU	Ben More Assynt. Cross-country from Kinloss. Wreck found by shepherd 26.05.41.	15/294232	L
18.08.42	DJ178	20 OTU	East Scaraben. Descended too soon on last leg of cross-country navex from Lossiemouth.	17/089282	S
24.04.44	AX435/ XF-S	19 OTU	Carn Na Cailliche. Hit hill in downdraught. All crew survived. Kinloss.	27/19-47-	X

AVRO LANCASTER

14.03.51	TX264/ BS-D	120 Sqn	Beinn Eighe. Night navex from Kinloss.	19/943601	L

Below: **Main undercarriage leg from the 19 OTU Anson N9857, which crashed on Ben More Assynt.**

BOEING FORTRESS

31.01.45	FL455 Z9-A	519 Sqn	Near Loch Rangag. Met flight from Wick..	11/142448	L

CONSOLIDATED B-24 LIBERATOR

18.08.44	BZ724/P	59 Sqn	Near Helmsdale. Diverting to Tain after anti-sub patrol from Ballykelly. Captain was sole survivor.	17/975152	S
13.06.45	42-95095	44th BG	Near Gairloch. Prestwick/Iceland.	19/809711-	M

DE HAVILLAND MOSQUITO

05.04.43	DZ486	618 Sqn	Cranstackie. Bombing exercise from Skitten.	9/559348	S

ENGLISH ELECTRIC CANBERRA

02.02.66	WT531	80 Sqn	Sron Garbh. Bruggen/Lossiemouth.	17/058261	L

FAIREY BARRACUDA

15/16.12.44	MX691/K	814 Sqn	Beinn nan Coireag. Six miles north-west of Berriedale. Night navex from Fearn. Probably cleared	17/12-25-	X
14.07.45	PM870	818 Sqn	Col Bheinn, Fearn.	17/886104	L

HANDLEY PAGE HAMPDEN

25.08.43	P2118/ Z9-D	519 Sqn	Ben Loyal. Returning to Wick from search for a missing Hampden.	10/583498	M

HAWKER HURRICANE

27.8.41	Z5145	331 Sqn	Near Westerdale. Crater and small pieces. Pilot baled out after collision.	11/177503	S

Below: **Sparse remains of Liberator V BZ724 near Helmsdale.** N J Perry

HAWKER SEA HAWK

| 04.09.57 | WV845 | AWTF | Near Brora. Lossiemouth. | 17/889080 | S |
| 05.05.59 | WM986/
616-LM | 736 Sqn | Findhorn. Lossiemouth. | 27/893336 | S |

MARTIN B-26 MARAUDER

| 03.06.43 | 41-34707 | 455BS/
322 BG | Beinn Na Feusaige. Ferrying Meeks Field (Iceland)/
Prestwick. | 25/038585 | S |

SHORT SUNDERLAND

| 25.08.42 | W4026/
M | 228 Sqn | Near Dunbeath. Invergordon/Iceland. 14 killed including HRH Duke
of Kent. Rear gunner survived. Memorial at site. | 17/110283 | |
| 15.08.44 | DP197 | 4 OTU | Creag Riabhach. Recalled to base at Alness due to weather
deterioration. 15 killed | | S |

VICKERS WELLINGTON

30.07.41	R1093	20 OTU	Carn Garbh. Navex from Lossiemouth.	17/895139	M
05.12.41	L4348	20 OTU	Near Tongue. Navex from Lossiemouth.	10/759457	M
14.02.42	N2825	20 OTU	Near Rothes. Navex from Lossiemouth.	28/?	M
14.11.43	HF746	20 OTU	Ben Rinnes. Navex from Lossiemouth.	27/257358	S

VOUGHT SIKORSKY VINDICATOR

| 23.04.42 | 1363 | VS-71 | Allt on Tor. Cleared early 1970s, only tiny pieces remain.
Flying Tain/Longman from USS *Wasp* in Scapa Flow. | 21/636773 | S |

Below: **Scattered wreckage of the Duke of Kent's Sunderland seen from a Hudson.**

Chapter Two

SCOTTISH ISLANDS

Aircraft remains on the islands represent a fair cross-section of wartime types. Strictly speaking, not all were as a result of collisions with high ground but have been included for interest. Salvage was not always possible for reasons of inaccessibility so wrecks were often broken up and buried where they had fallen. For example, bad weather and a four mile climb delayed the salvage of the Dakota IV on Mull and the majority of the aircraft was eventually dumped in a nearby ravine to render it invisible to overflying aircraft and thus avoid any further crash reports which would have to be investigated.

The Hebrides, Orkney and Shetland support a number of aerodromes, many of them built on far from ideal terrain at great expense in labour and materials and often dangerously close to high ground. They were, however, strategically essential to support Coastal Command operations, Trans-Atlantic ferrying and fighter cover for Scapa Flow, Loch Ewe and other naval bases. One of the few lasting social benefits of the war was a chain of airfields, more than adequate for post-war communications with the mainland.

Stornoway became an important staging post for short range aircraft ferrying through Iceland to Prestwick, its American-operated radio beacon serving also as a navigational aid for those overflying. Benbecula and Tiree were both used by Coastal Command for convoy escort duties and Port Ellen on Islay supported a Ferry Training Unit specialising in the Beaufighter, two being lost on the nearby hills. Sumburgh was another coastal base and flying-boat squadrons flew from Sullom Voe in the north of Shetland. Orkney had four

aerodromes, two of them for naval training at Hatston and Twatt, the others being fighter stations at Skeabrae and Kirkwall.

Most of the Orkney and Shetland wrecks have been visited since the last edition by enthusiasts David Hanson and John Finch-Davies. The Liberator GR.III on Hoy was not salvaged but its remains were dragged to the foot of the mountain and buried by the salvage team. On the Isle of Skye, the same was done with the B-17G which had hit Ben Edra, but much of it still lies in the rocky gullies.

I am told that the tail and engines from the Heinkel He 111 which crash-landed on Fair Isle were removed in recent years when an airstrip was built, but are still in the vicinity. On Foula, large sections of the Canadian Canso A amphibian were scattered across the small island by gales and much of it has now been cleared. The same fate befell the Oxford on Auskerry. Although it landed intact, it was totally demolished by a storm within days but parts may survive on the island.

On one of the most remote and forbidding island groups, that of St Kilda, are the remains of three aircraft. By coincidence they were all from Ferry Training Units which often used the islands as a turning point on navigational exercises. One of them is an unidentified Wellington which is almost certainly Mk.VIII LA995 of No.303 FTU, Stornoway which failed to return to base on 23rd February 1943. A comprehensive account of this and the other St Kilda accidents can be found in *After the Battle* magazine No.30.

The most southerly of the major Scottish islands is Arran, its jagged mountains ideally placed to trap unwary crews flying from Prestwick and other aerodromes in South-West Scotland. On Beinn Nuis the remains of three American aircraft lie within half a mile

of one another, parts of the B-17G Fortress still embedded in the cliff face where it impacted. The US Navy PBY4-1 Liberator almost made it to Prestwick from the USA but failed to clear the Beinn Nuis ridge by only a few feet. The identity of a nearby C-60 Lodestar is a mystery but it could have belonged to the 1403rd Base Unit at Prestwick or was even a US Navy R5O variant.

Another Arran wreck was LB-30A Liberator AM261 of the Atlantic Ferry Organisation. It had taken off from RAF Ayr for Gander and, despite a very experienced crew, failed to clear Am Binein, the adjacent mountain to the better-known Goat Fell. All 21 on board, many of them American and Canadian ferry crews, were killed and are buried at Lamlash. An Anson I crashed close to the Liberator the same year, but only small panels, some with trainer yellow paint, can be found.

The islands tend to resemble giant sponges and walking any great distance soon becomes tiring, particularly as paths are scarce. Some of the mountain ranges, on Skye, Jura and Arran to name but a few, are extremely rugged and expeditions should be planned accordingly.

Opposite page: **Outer wing of Vought Chesapeake AL941 on Arran.**

Below: **Distinctive wing root and wing folding mechanism of Corsair II JT461 on Hoy, Orkney.**
John Finch-Davies

AVRO ANSON
28.01.41	N4939	2 AONS	Am Binein, Arran. Navex from Prestwick.	69/00-42-	S
02.08.42	DJ472/45	1 OAFU	Caisteal Abhail, Arran. Navex from Wigtown.	69/967443-	S

BOEING B-17G FORTRESS
10.12.44	42-97286		Beinn Nuis, Arran. Knettishall/Prestwick.	69/957398	M
		388th BG			
03.03.45	44-83325	—	Beinn Edra, Skye. Ferrying Meeks Field/Valley.		
			Aircraft not assigned to a unit.	23/456630	M

BRISTOL BEAUFIGHTER
03.06.43	LX798	304 FTU	Conachair, St Kilda. Navex from Port Ellen.	18/099003	S
12 09.43	LX946	304 FTU	Mael Mheadhoin. Port Ellen	60/389520	S
12.09.43	LZ146	304 FTU	Near Port Ellen. In circuit area. Port Ellen.	60/?	S

BRISTOL BEAUFORT
30.08.42	L4479	5 OTU	Goat Fell, Arran. Navex from Turnberry.	69/987408	S
03.09.42	L9803/Y	TTU	Ben More, Mull Navex from Abbotsinch.	48/523334	M

BRISTOL BLENHEIM
03.09.41	L9261	235 Sqn	Sandness Hill,, Shetland. Sumburgh.	3/189562-	X
21.02.42	V5433	404 Sqn	Grundy, Out Skerries. Sumburgh	2/695713	L

CHANCE VOUGHT CORSAIR
11.07.44	JT461/7C	1841 Sqn	Enegars, Hoy. Hatston/HMS *Formidable*.	7/198042	M

CONSOLIDATED CATALINA
15.07.41	AH533	210 Sqn	Jura. Patrol from Oban.	61/687984	S
19.01.42	Z2148	240 Sqn	Yell, Shetland. Circling at night waiting for flarepath to be changed. Loch Erne/Sullom Voe.	3/481852	M
12 05.44	JX273	302 FTU	Vatersay. Navex from Oban.	31/641957	L

CONSOLIDATED CANSO
29.07 44	11062	162 Sqn	Foula. Anti-sub patrol from Wick.	4/948396	M

CONSOLIDATED LIBERATOR
10.08.41	AM261	ATFERO	Am Binein, Arran. Ayr/Gander. 21 killed.	69/992425	S
20.08.43	42-41030	Knox	Beinn Nuis, Arran. US Navy PBY4-1. Ferrying Iceland/		
		Prov Group	Prestwick.	69/957396	M
15.09.43	4Z-72851	–	North Lee, North Uist. Ferrying Iceland/Nutts Corner	18/929665	M
01.01.45	FL949/Y	311 Sqn	Hoy. Mostly buried by MU. Patrol from Tain.	7/208030	M

DE HAVILLAND MOSQUITO
22.11.44	DZ642	627 Sqn	Royal Field Hill, Shetland	4/392284-	L

DOUGLAS DAKOTA
01.02.45	KK194	45 Gp	Ben Talaidh, Mull. Ferrying Iceland/Prestwick.	48/625359	L

FAIREY ALBACORE
26.06.42	BF592	Evanton FF	Mel Fea, Hoy. Evanton/Hatson.	7/210975	L

Above: **Port wing from B-24D Liberator 42-41030 on Beinn Nuis, Arran. The early-type insignia is outlined in red.** David Sutherland

FAIREY BARRACUDA

02.01.45	LS931	815 Sqn	Beinn an Orr, Jura, Ayr.	61/495745	M
16.04.45	MX794	837 Sqn	Goat Fell, Arran. Navex from HMS *Glory*.	69/99-42-	X

FAIREY FIREFLY

25.09.51	WB336	719 Sqn	Beinn Uraraioth, Islay. Training flt from Eglinton.	60/408542	L

GENERAL DYNAMICS F-111F

07.12.82	70-2377	48 TFW	Na Stri, Skye . Lakenheath.	32/50-19-	S

GRUMMAN MARTLET

04.06.43	FN284	878 Sqn	Orkney. Night training flight from Hatston.		X
04.06.43	FN288	878 Sqn	Orkney. Night trainingflight from Hatston.		X

HANDLEY PAGE HALIFAX

31.03.42	R9438/ TL-H	35 Sqn	Whales Wlck, Fitful Head, Shetland. Diverting to Sumburg after raid on *Tirpitz* from Kinloss. Inaccessible and now a war grave.	4/343134	
09.04.45	JP165/D	58 Sqn	Beinn Nan Leac, Harris. Met sortie from Stornoway.	14/128984	M

HAWKER HUNTER

12.02.80	XK151/Z	2 TWU	Bla Bheinn, Skye.	32/53-22-	X

HAWKER HURRICANE

06.02.44	LF207	516 Sqn	Coll. On combined operations exercise from Connel.	46/?	S

HEINKEL He 111

| 17.01.41 | 2645/ | Wekusta | Fair Isle. Tail and engines still in situ. | |
| | T5+EU | Od d L | Probably from Stavanger. | 4/214718 |

LOCKHEED HUDSON

| 19.03.41 | N7310 | 220 Sqn | Wiht Gill, Hoy. On patrol from Wick. | 6/252962 | L |
| 31.07.42 | FH375/W | 500 Sqn | Lewis. Air test from Stornoway. | 8/? | L |

LOCKHEED C-60 LODESTAR

| ?.12.43 | | 1403rd BU? | Beinn Nuis, Arran. Prestwick? | 69/956401 | S |

SHORT SUNDERLAND

| 08.06.44 | ML858 | 302 FTU | St Kilda. Navex from Oban. | 18/096998 | L |

SUPERMARINE SEAFIRE

| 19.06.43 | NM940 | 886 Sqn | Auchdreoch, Arran. Machrihanish. Area now afforested. | 69/99-24- | X |

SUPERMARINE SPITFIRE

23.09.41	X4108	124 Sqn	Rendall, Orkney. Convoy escort from Castletown.	6/?	X
19.06.43	R7198	8 OTU	Skye. Cross-country from Dyce.	23 or 33/?	X
06.04.45	TB914	329 Sqn	Skelday Hill, Orkney. Skeabrae.	6/32-34-	S

VICKERS WELLINGTON

| 23.02.43? | LA995? | 303 FTU? | Soay, St Kilda. Almost definately LA995 lost in this area on navex from Stornoway. | | M |

VOUGHT SIKORSKY CHESAPEAKE

| 22.07.43 | AL941 | 772 Sqn | Glen Catacol, Arran. Exercise from Machrihanish. | 69/93-46- | M |

Chapter Three

CENTRAL SCOTLAND

Taking a line through the Firths of Forth and Clyde as its southern extremity, this region encompasses the Cairngorms, Grampians, Trossachs and several lesser known ranges. The largest number of wrecks is to be found on the Grampians in the vicinity of Glen Clova, Glen Esk and Glen Isla. Further to the north west are the Cairngorms which contain relatively few crash sites. Despite their inaccessibility, the aircraft are very broken up and rather disappointing. Only the very experienced should venture into this rugged country. Some of the wrecks ideally require a two-day expedition.

Wellingtons and Whitleys from Lossiemouth and Kinloss are scattered throughout the Highlands and the training aerodrome at Montrose saw many Masters and Oxfords take off never to return. Two of the aircraft lost in the mountains seem to have been missing for the longest period of any high ground crash in Britain, apart from the Spitfire on the Brecon Beacons (qv). One was Oxford I PH404 found by climbers seven months after it vanished, the other was a Master II from Montrose, AZ333, missing for nearly eight months and also discovered by chance.

No further information has come to light to confirm or deny the legend of the Sopwith Camel wreck in the Grampians. The Albemarle I near Kenmore was probably on low ground and was being flown by a Russian crew who were training on the type before delivering a batch of them to the USSR. The F-101C Voodoo on Maol Odhar was missing for more than a week, during which an intensive air search was mounted using Prest-

wick as a base. The unprecedented efforts gave rise to speculation that it was carrying something sensitive, but nothing was ever admitted publicly.

The rarely visited Monadhliath Mountains contain the remains of a Lancaster I which disintegrated in mid-air, spreading wreckage over several miles. Another Lancaster, a Mk.III, broke up near Loch Lomond, some pieces falling to earth on Conic Hill. The same fate appears to have befallen the Halifax V in Glen Isla.

The Youth Hostel in Glen Affric probably still uses parts of a crashed Wellington IC for various domestic functions. The aircraft plunged into the glen after the crew baled out during a night exercise. They were unable to maintain height after one engine failed over the mountains and a forced-landing attempt would have been suicidal. A Wellington IC from the same unit flew into Ben Alder at a position so far from a road that salvage would appear to have been impossible. To the annoyance of a later generation of aviation archaeologists, an Indian Army unit training in the area removed it piecemeal with pack mules!

The Mosquito Mk.6 in Glen Esk was flying the celebrated Stockholm courier service when it disappeared while returning to Leuchars after an engine failure. A month later the wreckage was found by a gamekeeper. The stream at the head of which it had crashed is known locally as the 'Mosquito Burn' and perhaps this name will one day find its way onto the OS Map. Another aircraft of some historical importance crashed in the Ochil Hills above Alloa in 1941. It was Liberator I AM926 which had taken part in several recent actions against U-boats. The fighter OTU at Grangemouth lost three Spitfires in the Ochils but no trace of either these or the Liberator have yet been found.

The burned-out remains of the B-29A near Lochgoilhead are a sad and sobering sight. All 20 on board were killed and the largest parts of the wreck are an outer wing, the tail turret, two engines and the massive undercarriage forgings. A fine memorial has now been dedicated on the site. A few miles away can be found the quite large pieces of an early Grumman Martlet I.

The Whitley I which crashed near Balquhidder in November 1940 was once one of Scotland's most interesting wrecks. When I went to it in 1968 it was all there apart from the burned-out front fuselage. Since then it has been progressively pillaged, both privately and by service personnel. A propeller was set up at th Forest Centre at Strathyre as a memorial to the crew, but I am not sure if it is still there . The rear gunner was the sole survivor and local legend has it that he hid for several days believing that he was in enemy territory. This tale is told about other crash survivors, however!

Below: **Remains of 217 Squadron Beaufort I AW242 on Wirren.** John Caie

AIRSPEED OXFORD

Date	Serial	Unit	Location / Notes	Grid	
31.01.40	N6320	15 SFTS	Glen Buchat. Navex from Lossiemouth.	37/?	X
02.03.42	L4597	45 MU	Loch Laidon. Engines now recovered.		
			Ferrying Cambridge/Kinloss.	41/390545	S
03.09.42	N6438	2 FIS	Meluncart. Montrose.	43/629819	S
12.10.43	HM724	19 PAFU	Braeriach. Sucked onto mountain top by downdraught.		
			Crew unhurt but had a long walk! Dalcross	36/960005	S
26.10.44	DF448	2 FIS	Shank of Donald Young. Navex from Montrose.	44/42-74-	X
10.01.45	PH404	311 Sqn	Bheinn A 'Bhuird. Somewhere in England/Tain.		
			Wreck found by climbers	36/112025	M
24.08.50	PH311	66 Gp CF	Cairn Trench.Turnhouse/Dyce.	44/391736	S

ARMSTRONG WHITWORTH ALBEMARLE

Date	Serial	Unit	Location / Notes	Grid	
29.05.43	P1503	305 FTU	Near Kenmore Probably cleared. On navex from Errol.		
			Russian crew killed.	52/?	X

ARMSTRONG WHITWORTH WHITLEY

Date	Serial	Unit	Location / Notes	Grid	
01.05.40	N1500	102 Sqn	Hill of Foudland. Kinloss/Leuchars.	29/608338	S
24.11.40	P5090/L	502 Sqn	Fathan Glinne. Lost returning to Aldergrove from anti-sub patrol.	57/474169	M
23/24.03.42	Z6933/Z	19 OTU	Finalty Hill.Kinloss.Wreck found 05.06.42.	44/215762	M
31.01.43	LA837/F	19 OTU	Cromdale Hills. On navex from Kinloss.	36/140295	X
03.07.43	LA877/W	19 OTU	Meallan Odhar. Engine failure on night bombing practice from Kinloss.	36/527806	M
26.05.44	EB384/U	19 OTU	Glen Esk A wing almost intact. Navex from Kinloss.	44/324808	M

AVRO ANSON

Date	Serial	Unit	Location / Notes	Grid	
07.08.41	R9584/ ZT-J	20 OTU	Glen Avon. Seen to dive into hill, possibility of sabotage to elevator controls. Eight killed. Elgin/Turnhouse.	36/?	X
21.08.42	DJ106	19 OTU	Ben McDhui. Navex from Kinloss. Memorial on site	43/986992	M

AVRO LANCASTER

Date	Serial	Unit	Location / Notes	Grid	
31.08.44	PD258/ JO-G	463 Sqn	Monadhliath Mts. Mid-air break up whilst returning to Waddington from ops, Konigsberg.	37/725106	S
13.09.44	PB456	101 Sqn	Conic Hill. Mid-air break up on navex from Ludford Magna.	56/420932	S

AVRO VULCAN

Date	Serial	Unit	Location / Notes	Grid	
12.06.63	XH477	44 Sqn	Hill of St Colm. Training flight from Finningley.	44/493884	S

BLACKBURN ROC

Date	Serial	Unit	Location / Notes	Grid	
01.10.41	L3073	772 Sqn	Near Airdo Farm, Crinan. Machrihanish..	55/76-99-	X

BOEING B-29 SUPERFORTRESS

Date	Serial	Unit	Location / Notes	Grid	
17.01.49	44-62276	301st BG	Succoth Glen. 20 killed Scampton/Keflavik.	56/161022	L

BRISTOL BEAUFIGHTER

Date	Serial	Unit	Location / Notes	Grid	
03.03.43	EL335/P	235 Sqn	Six miles north west of Edzell. Leuchars.	44/?	X

BRISTOL BEAUFORT

Date	Serial	Unit	Location / Notes	Grid	
08.03.42	AW242	217Sqn	Wirren. Leuchars/Wick.	44/515739	M

BRISTOL BLENHEIM

06.04.41	L1500	141 Sqn	Gargunnock Hills. Crash-landing. Crew survived. Ayr.	57/69-92-	X
10.12.41	V5801/QY-P	254 Sqn	Glen Isla. Aldergrove/Dyce.	44/?	X
19.10.43	T1863	526 Sqn	Morven. Base was Inverness.	37/386046	S
26.03 .45	Z7356	526 Sqn	Braeriach. Descended too soon to break cloud. Digby/Longman	36/960005	M

CESSNA 150

17.11.81	G-BFHL	–	Ben Ledi. Inverness/Glasgow.	57/56-10-	X

CONSOLIDATED LIBERATOR

10.12.41	AM926/ OH-F	120 Sqn	Tarmangie Hill. This aircraft had made the squadron's first attack on a U-boat on 22.10.41. Dyce/Nutts Corner.	58/94-01-	X
17.10.44	KG857	547 Sqn	Wirren. On anti-sub patrol. Captain and three others survived. Leuchars.	44/521733	M

DE HAVILLAND MOSQUITO

17.08.43	G-AGGF	BOAC	Glen Esk. Returning due to malfunction. Found by gamekeeper 08.09.43 . Leuchars/Stockholm.	44/351806	M

DE HAVILLAND TIGER MOTH

30.10.42	?	11 EFTS	Near Kippen. Crew walked 4½ miles to safety. Perth.	57/?	X
17.10.44	T5466	11 EFTS	Three miles north west of Fettercairn. Perth.	45/?	X
29.08.57	G-AKCH		Blainenon. Engine only. Perth/Donibristle.	58/863019	

ENGLISH ELECTRIC CANBERRA

22.11.56	WJ615	50 Sqn	Carn An t'Sagairt Mor. Kinloss/Upwood.	44/206845	L

FAIREY ALBACORE

01.05.41	N4305	767 Sqn	Glen Clova Arbroath.	44/277784	M
31.05.43	L7138	9 PAFU	Five miles north of Clova Inn. Forced-landing, presumed recovered. Errol.	44/?	X

FAIREY BARRACUDA

28.05.44	LS520	831 Sqn	Nr Amulree, Perthshire. Machrihanish/Hatston	52/90-36-	X

FAIREY FIREFLY

16.05.49	Z2108/ 245-LM	766 Sqn	Lochnagar. Yellow painted wreckage visible from a distance. Lossiemouth.	44/263848	L

FAIREY SWORDFISH

–	L9730	786 Sqn?	Glen Callater. Complete in a heap. From Arbroath?	44/204801	
15.12.40	K5949	767 Sqn	Glen Prosen. Mainly wing parts. Training flight from Arbroath.	44/323706	S
14.09.42	L9785	769 Sqn	Hill of Wirren. Arbroath	44/52-74-	X

GLOSTER METEOR

12.02.52	WA882	222 Sqn	Benachie. Low flying exercise from Leuchars.	38/663220	S

GRUMMAN MARTLET

13.12.40	AL251	FLR	Ben Bheula. Abbotsinch/Donibristle.	56/157983	M

Above: **The Airspeed Oxford was mainly of wooden construction, so only metal fittings tend to survive at crash sites. N6438 lying on Meluncart in the Grampians.**

Below: **Air Training Corps cadets examining the remains of Lancaster I PD258 in the Monadhliath Mountains. Part of the 463 Squadron code 'JO-G' can be discerned.** J Gibbons via Jim Hughes

Above: **B-29A 44-62276 tail turret and tail bumper hydraulic ram. A fine memorial to the 20 occupants has now been dedicated at the site.**

Below: **Outer wing of Martlet I AL251 with faded roundel on Ben Bheula.**

HANDLEY PAGE HALIFAX

01.06.44	LL414	1667 HCU	Glen Isla. Cross-country from Sandtoft.	43/190740	S

HAWKER AUDAX

05.05.39	K7376	8 FTS	Edendocher Hill. Local flight from Montrose. Two crew survived.	45/606852	S
05.02.40	K7473	8 FTS	Cairn O'Mount. Montrose.	45/663806	S

HAWKER FURY

18.01.38	K8263	8 FTS	Tipperweir Hill. Local flight from Montrose. Pilot survived.	45/69-86-	S

HAWKER HENLEY

01.05.40	L3303	8 BGS	Eight miles south of Huntly. Off track in bad visibility. Evanton.	37/?	X

HAWKER HURRICANE

05.12.40	P3470	111 Sqn	Ten miles NW of Edzell. Ferrying Drem/Montrose.	44/?	X
09.08.42	AG164	56 OTU	Near Loch Rannoch. Broke away from formation, possibly owing to lack of oxygen. Tealing.	42/?	X
04.10.42	AF978	56 OTU	Wirren. Formation practice from Tealing.	44/52-73-	X
21.04.43	V6938	56 OTU	Bawhelps. Local flight from Tealing.	44/230720	S
19.11.43	BE651 and HV840	1 TEU	Cleish Hill. Formation practice, got into cloud and lost leader. Tealing.	58/08-96-	X
06.02.44	LF160	516 Sqn	Near Kilchoan. On combined operations exercise from Connel.	47/464638	S

HAWKER SEA FURY

16.09.53	VW590/ 108-J	811 Sqn	East Wirren. Arbroath.	44/558732	S

LOCKHEED 14

22.04.40	G-AFKD	–	Ben Uird. Perth/Heston.	56/40-98-	S

LOCKHEED HUDSON

15.04.41	T9432	233 Sqn	Ben Lui. Anti-sub patrol from Aldergrove.	50/273264	L

McDONNELL F-101 VOODOO

07.05.64	56-0013	81 TFW	Maol Odhar.Bentwaters.	49/883578	S

MILES MAGISTER

16.09.40	T9814	19 OTU	Six miles south of Dalwhinnie. Kinloss.	42/?	X

MILES MASTER

27.04.41	N7511	8 FTS	Forest of Birse. Lost in bad weather. Montrose.	44/53-91-	X
01.10.41	T8383	8 FTS	Pinderachy Hill. Navex from Montrose.	44/46-65-	X
09.10.41	T8684	8 FTS	Cairn of Fingleny. Navex from Montrose.	45/615847	M
17.01.42	AZ263	8 FTS	Tillentirk Hill. Navex from Montrose.	45/?	X
15.12.42	N7602	8 FTS	Hill of Fingray. Montrose	44/572816	S
18.03.43	DL415	2 FIS	Nathro Lodge. Navex from Montrose.	44/50-69-	X
24.11.43	AZ333	2 FIS	Grampians. Cross-country from Montrose. Found 11.07.44.	44/?	X

NORTH AMERICAN HARVARD
06.09.54   KF177   3 FTS   Craigancash. Kinloss/Leuchars.   44/584775   X

NORTH AMERICAN F-86 SABRE
05.04.53   XB610   147 Sqn   Glen Gheallaidh Burn..   28/12-39-   S

NORTH AMERICAN F-100D SUPER SABRE
07.08.69   55-2817   48 TFW   Peter Hill. Low-level cross-country from Lakenheath.
    Pilot ejected.   44/589899   X

SEPECAT JAGUAR
23.11.79   XX762/28   226 OCU   Beinn A'Chleibh. Lossiemouth.   50/25-27-   X

SUPERMARINE SCIMITAR
10.11.59   XD281/   807 Sqn   Ben Vorlich. Pilot ejected. Lossiemouth.
    190-R   57/620163   S

SUPERMARINE SPITFIRE
10.03.41   X4647   58 OTU   Ben Ledi. Lost without radio. Northolt/Grangemouth. 57/56-10-   X
01.07.41   X4318   58 OTU   Cloon. Grangemouth.   58/038047   S
26.09.41   R6983   58 OTU   Ben Gengie. Local flight from Grangemouth.   58/87-00-   X
17.10.41   X4904   58 OTU   Ochills. Formation practice from Grangemouth.   58/?   X
05.11.42   R6886   8 OTU   Glen Truim. Cockpit filled with smoke. Pilot baled out.
    Fraserburgh.   35/?   S
10.11.42   X4487   8 OTU   Glen Clova.   44/350700   S
10.06.43   X4241   58 OTU   Maddie Moss. Grangemouth.   58/93-01-   X

SUPERMARINE WALRUS
10.08.43   W3023   751 Sqn   Glen Turret. Dundee   52/81-27-   X

VICKERS WELLINGTON
19.09.40   N2883   20 OTU   Glen Moriston. Navex from Lossiemouth.   34/?   X
23.10.40   L7775   20 OTU   Bruach Mor. Misjudged position and let down too
    soon on navex from Lossiemouth .   43/089964   S
13.02.42   T2707/   20 OTU   Glen Affric. One engine failed, unable to maintain
    JM-Z   height over mountains at night. Crew baled out.
    Lossiemouth/Tiree.   34/076195   M
10.12.42   L7867/   20 OTU   Ben Alder. Navex from Lossiemouth.
    JM-J   Much of wreckage salvaged with pack mules.   42/480732   S

WESTLAND WALLACE
03 09.39   K6028   9 AOS   Benachie. Ferrying Evanton/Dyce.   38/668716   M

Chapter Four

SOUTHERN SCOTLAND

There are two notable concentrations of wrecks in this part of Scotland; the Mull of Kintyre and the Cairnsmore of Fleet. Both rear from the sea in ideal positions to trap unwary flyers and consequently became graveyards of aircraft. Another forbidding location lies to the west of Newton Stewart. It is wild, remote and beautiful but generally overlooked by people intent on speeding north to the Highlands. The long hikes to the wreck sites are amply rewarded by the scenery. The same can be said for the lonely rolling hills between the border and Edinburgh which include the Lammermuirs and the Moffat Hills.

Operational flying over the region was confined mainly to fighter squadrons based at Ayr, Drem, Abbotsinch and Turnhouse. A chain of airfields along the coast supported a variety of training activities safe from enemy interference but not from the effects of weather and high ground. Torpedo attack techniques were taught at Turnberry and Castle Kennedy, aerial gunnery at West Freugh, navigation at Wigtown and Dumfries, and Annan was a fighter OTU. RAF Dumfries doubled as an important MU and Aircraft Storage Unit.

Prestwick, perhaps the best-known Scottish airfield, was the terminal for a large proportion of all the thousands of aircraft ferried across the Atlantic for the RAF and USAAF. Although its weather record is excellent, there is much high ground in the vicinity and the tragic consequences of navigational errors can be seen to this day.

Prestwick was still a useful staging point well after the war and the B-26 Invader on the Blackside Hills was on its way via Iceland to join the French Air Force. A P-47 Thunderbolt on the same hill was salvaged by the RAF after the USAAF found its heavy vehicles totally unsuitable for the job.

The huge bulk of the Cairnsmore of Fleet took a terrible toll of training aircraft, but unfortunately it is impossible to differentiate between the five Anson crashes as there are only sparse remains at the impact points. The impressive tail of the Heinkel He111 has now been recovered for preservation and much of the other wreckage was brought down by a USAF HH-53 'Super Jolly' helicopter when a memorial plaque to all the aircrew killed on the mountain was placed on the summit by the Dumfries & Galloway Aviation Group. The tail and undercarriage now reside with the North East Aircraft Museum at Usworth.

The Mull of Kintyre seems to have been another magnet for aircraft, lying as it did on navigation exercise routes and close to the anti-submarine bases in Northern Ireland. Long after the war it claimed two more Coastal Command aircraft, a Neptune MR.1 and Shackleton MR.2. The latter was salvaged almost in its entirety but the Neptune was left more or less as it crashed with large sections strewn over the hill.

The hills to the east of Largs in Ayrshire are not particularly high but possess a surprisingly large number of crash sites. Potential investigators are warned that a compass is essential even on a clear day to identify the numerous small hills which all look alike.

One of the most interesting relics up here was the fuselage of the three-engined Spartan Cruiser III G-ACYK now in the Museum of Flight at East Fortune. Close to where the Cruiser crash-landed is a badly broken up Seafire XV and on Box Law an RAF Devon C.1 which, when seen in 1969 from the

Viking 3B wreck a mile away, appeared to be complete. It was only when we reached it that we found that the fuselage had been salvaged. The occupants of the Cruiser, Viking and Devon all escaped serious injury.

There were many collisions with the moorland around Lochwinnoch, but access was fairly easy and they were almost definitely removed. In the 1950s I am told there was a Typhoon wing in use as a gate on a farm in this area. It may have come from Mk.IB DN365 but I am unaware of its exact location, assuming it still exists. Further north, near Greenock, an engine from the Anson I on Dunrod hill forms a memorial at the Country Park Centre.

A wreck which still defies identification is a Fairchild Argus on a hilltop in the Moffat area. The cockpit structure and struts confirm the type and, according to local people,

the occupants all escaped unscathed. It has been suggested that it was a civilian aircraft which crashed around 1950. RAF wartime records show no relevant Argus loss but it could also be a USAAF UC-61.

The ANEC Missel Thrush on Broad Law was a small low-winged monoplane which crashed on the Newcastle–Glasgow leg of the King's Cup Air Race, which in those days was a long distance affair. I am told that the engine remains on the mountain. The unknown wreck on Wester Dodd near Berwick is not Halifax II JP190 of No.1656 HCU reported crashed on 'Wolf Cleugh Head' on 1st April 1944. I have now discovered Wolf Cleugh is near Hawick. Another mystery surrounds the Seafire on Merrick. Contemporary newspapers report that it belonged to the Royal Canadian Navy but it would appear that this was pure conjecture.

Below: **The mystery Fairchild Argus forward cockpit frame and port undercarriage leg on a hilltop in the Moffat area. It steadfastly defies positive identification.**

ANEC MISSEL THRUSH

20.07.28	G-EBRI		Broad Law. Competitor in King's Cup Air Race. Cramlington/Renfrew.	72/15-24-	S

AIRSPEED OXFORD

15.03.42	X7190	6 FPP	Near Wigtown. Ferrying Ratcliffe/Edzell.	83/?	X
17.08.42	?	TTU	Near Strathaven. Prestwick.	64/?	X

ARMSTRONG WHIITWORTH WHITLEY

23.01.41	P5041	502 Sqn	Mull of Kintyre. Became lost after convoy escort duty. Aldergrove.	68/597095	S

AUSTER WORKMASTER

18.10.63	G-APMJ		Dungeon Hill. Crosby-on-Eden/Campbeltown.	77/457862	M

AVRO ANSON

03.02.37	K6252	269 Sqn	Two miles from Leadhills searching for DH.90 Dragonfly G-AEHC.	71/?	X
19.09.38	L7949	12 E&R FTS	Misty Law. Navex from Prestwick.	63/29-62	X
09.01.39	L9153	1 CANS	Rhinns of Kells. Night navex from Prestwick.	77/?	X
26.07.39	K6255/ UA-A	269 Sqn	Dunrod Hill. Hit hill-top formation flying. Three survivors. From Abbotsinch.	63/237730	S
17.04.42	W2630	1 OAFU	Cairnsmore. Navex from Wigtown.	86/?	X
02.07.42	N5297	2 OAFU	Shalloch-on-Minnoch. Navex from Millom.	77/407907	S
22.09.42	DJ126	9 OAFU	Cairnsmore. Navex from Llandwrog.	83/?	X
23.10.42	DG787/J	ANBS	Corserine. Navex from Jurby.	77/49?873	S
03.02.43	N4995	1 OAFU	Cairn Hill. Navex from Wigtown.	76/?	X
10.10.43	EF820	9 OAFU	Mull of Kintyre. Navex from Llandwrog.	68/?	X
22.02.44	EG485/L1	10 OAFU	Cairnsmore. Navex from Dumfries.	83/?	X
12.06.44	N9589	4 OAFU	Cairnsmore. Navex from West Freugh.	83/?	X
09.07.44	N5140	1 OAFU	Knocktim, Cairnsmore. Navex from Wigtown.	83/50-64-	X
21.07.44	MG356	4 OAFU	Bennanbrackie. Navex from West Freugh.	77/440775	M
04.11.44	MG827	10 OAFU	Criffell. Navex from Dumfries. Crew survived.	84/953622	M
06.12.44	EG693/65	2 OAFU	Craigronald. Navex from Millom.	83/523690	M
01.02.45	NK945	45 MU	Turf Law. Kinloss/?	66/47-56-	X

AVRO SHACKLETON

19.04.68	WB833/T	210 Sqn	Glenanuilt Hill. On exercise from Ballykelly.	68/649074	S

BEECHCRAFT TRAVELER

22.12.44	FT529	725 Sqn	Near Campbeltown. Kintyre. Based Eglinton.	77/?	X

BLACKBURN BOTHA

02.03.42	L6539	10 AOS	Cairnsnmore. Navex from Dumfries.	83/503668	X

BOULTON PAUL DEFIANT

29.08.41	T4042	60 OTU	Hunt Law. Loss of control in cloud. East Fortune. Pilot's grave on site.	73/573577	S
30.08.41	N1731	410 Sqn	Bleak Law.Training flight from Drem.	66/53-61-	X
15.10.41	N1739	60 OTU	Five miles S of Gifford. Crew survived. East Fortune.	63/?	X

BRISTOL BEAUFIGHTER

21.07.42	X7764	4 FPP	Auchingilloch. Ferrying Dumfries/Lossiemouth.	71/706360	S
28.08.43	LZ156	304 FTU	Mull of Kintyre. Cross-country from Port Ellen.	68/624063	S
30.10.43	LZ455	2 OAPU	Beinn Bhreac. Ferrying Filton to ?	68/615087	S
03.05.45	NE813	132 OTU	Near Oldhamstocks. From East Fortune.	67/702699	S

BRISTOL BEAUFORT

27.10.41	L9817	TTU	Knockside Hill. Torpedo exercise from Abbotsinch.	63/26-58-	X
02.09.42	N1180/S	TTU	Tor Mhor. Exercise from Abbotsinch.	68/598079	S

BRISTOL BLENHEIM

08.11.39	P4848	SD Flt	Ben Inner. Perth/St Athan.	77/612968	M
03.07.41	Z5871	60 OTU	Lammermuir Hills. East Fortune	73/?	
30.07.41	Z7646	18 MU	Blackhope Scar. Ferrying Haddington/Dumfries.	73/31-48-	X
21.12.41	Z6350	5 AOS	Mull of Kintyre. Navex from Jurby.	68/?	X
05.04.43	BA741	42 OTU	Near Peebles. Cross-country from Ashbourne.	72/?	X
09.05.44	V5795	527 Sqn	Hart Fell. Inverness/Digby.	72/11-13-	X

CONSOLIDATED CATALINA

30.12.42	FP184	131 OTU	Smyrton Hill. Navex from Killadeas.	76/12-79--	S

CONSOLIDATED B-24 LIBERATOR

31.08.41	AM915	BOAC	Arinardch Hill. Gander/Prestwick. Wreck marker located at 68/733157.	68/737158	S
14.09.42	AL624	1653 HCU	Millfore.Training flight Prestwick/Burn.	77/471749	M
12.06.45	44-50695	448thBG	Goodman's Cairn. Seething/Prestwick.	76/134778	S

DE HAVILLAND DEVON

03.06.58	VP969	MCCF	Box Law. Andover/Renfrew.	63/258607	L

DE HAVILLAND DOMINIE

28.02.49	X7400	782 Sqn	Dun Rig Peebleshire. There are several mountains of this name!	X

DE HAVILLAND DH.90 DRAGONFLY

02.02.37	G-AEHC	–	Cairn Darnaw. Memorial at site. Renfrew/Speke.	77/516766	S

DE HAVILLAND DRAGON RAPIDE

27.09.46	G-AFFF	–	Craigton Hill. Islay (Port Ellen)/Renfrew.	64/511769	S

DE HAVILLAND DH 60 MOTH

26.09.36	G-ACGD	–	Dollar Law. Edinburgh Flying Club, Turnhouse.	72/181277-	M

DE HAVILLAND MOSQUITO

21.01.44	DD795	60 OTU	Corserine. Night navex from High Ercall.	77/504870	M

DE HAVILLAND TIGER MOTH

10.01.39	L6932	12 E&RFTS	Rhinns of Kells. Searching for a missing Anson. Crew uninjured and wreck salvaged. Prestwick.	77/?	
26.05.40	N9202	2 CPF	Ladyland Moor. Abbotsinch.	63/30-59-	X

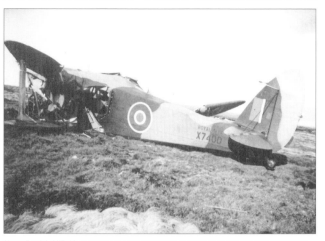

Above: **Dominie I X7400 shortly after its crash on Dun Rig. Everybody walked away from the accident.**

Below: **DH.90 Dragonfly G-AEHC crashed on Cairn Darnaw while en route Renfrew to Speke in 1937. A few pieces of wreckage can be found beside the memorial which marks the crash site.**

DORNIER Do 217E-4
25.03.43   4365   7/KG2   Carnharrow. Based in Holland.   83/53-56-   X

DOUGLAS HAVOC
03.08.41   AH463   14 FPP   Near New Cumnock. Ferrying Abbotsinch/Burtonwood. 71/?   X

DOUGLAS B-26 INVADER
16.08.56   '8811B'   Fr AF   Distinkhorn. Instrument let down into Prestwick from Keflavik on delivery.   71/594332 M

DOUGLAS DAKOTA
10.04.47   K-14   RBel AF   Carlin's Cairn. Brussels-Evere/Prestwick.   77/498881/502882 M
28.03.56   G-AMRB Starways   Greenside Hill. Speke/Renfrew.   63/28-58-   X

FAIREY BATTLE
29.09.41   L4997   10 AOS   Lamb Hill. Loss of control in cloud. Dumfries.   78/954935 S

FAIREY FIREFLY
26.10.44   DT977/4A1770 Sqn   Blaeloch Hill. Training exercise from Ayr.   63/239550 M
08.01.50   PP566/ 1830 Sqn   Meikle Bin. Local flight from Abbotsinch   64/668822 L
           208-AC

FAIREY FULMAR
07.07.41   N4038–   804 Sqn   Kerran Hill, Kintyre. HMS *Pegasus*/Aldergrove.   68/73-13-   X
27.04.44   X8751–   772 Sqn   Near Black Loch. Machrihanish.   68/79-39--   X

FAIREY SWORDFISH
30.01.42   V4554   823 Sqn   Calder Dam. Fraserburgh/Machrihanish.   63/29-65-   X
08.12.43   HS274   860 Sqn   Near Carron Bridge. Based Maydown.   64/65-82--   X

GENERAL DYNAMICS F-111E
19.12.79   68-0003   20 TFW   Craignaw. Upper Heyford   83/458832- S

GLOSTER JAVELIN
21.11.60   XA825/K   29 Sqn   Bowbeat Hill. Leuchars.   73/295475 M

GRUMMAN AVENGER
28.05.44   FN867   852 Sqn   Two miles north west of Carradale. Machrihanish   68/79-39-   X
04.07.44   FN772   768 Sqn   Black Loch Hill. Abbotsinch.   68/79-39--   X

GRUMMAN HELLCAT
07.08.45   JX966   892 Sqn   Near Brothershiels Farm. Fala Moor..   -
           Night flying navex from Drem   66/42-56--- X

GRUMMAN WILDCAT
02.12.44   JV499   778 Sqn   Blackside. Ayr/Arbroath.   71/598298 S
11.09.45   JV404   898 Sqn   Palgowan Farm, Bargrennan. Stretton/Ayr.   76/34-78-   X

HANDLEY PAGE HALIFAX
01.04.44   JP190 1656 HCU   Wolf Cleugh Head, near Hawick. Navex from Lindholme. 79/325079 X

Above: **Tail unit from Wildcat V JV499 on Blackside. Sadly, a local farmer pulled it off the hill with a tractor and sold it for scrap.** Peter Quaile

HANDLEY PAGE HAMPDEN

18.01.44	P1216	BTU	Braid Fell. Stalled, dived into ground. West Freugh.	82/11-67-	X

HAWKER HIND

07.04.37	K6634	83 Sqn	Queensbury Hill. Cross-country from Turnhouse.	78/988997	S
30.01.42	K6838	4 FPP	Eaglesham Moor. Ferrying Lossiemouth/Prestwick.	64/55-51-	X

HAWKER HURRICANE

21.07.41	W9112	59 OTU	Lowther Hills. Crosby-on-Eden.	71/?	X
13.09.43	KZ398 and		Shalloch-on-Minnoch. Training flight from Ayr.		
	KZ674	186 Sqn		77/40-91-	X
18.03.44	LD564	439 Sqn	Loch Doon. Dived out of cloud Ayr.	77/492923	S

HAWKER SEA HURRICANE

12.09.42	JS346	16 FP	Near Ewes Lees Farm. Langholm. Kirkbride/Arbroath Pilot was Prince Chirosakti of Siam	79/38-98-	S

HAWKER TYPHOON

24.01.43	DN365	197 Sqn	Near Lochwinnoch. Drem.	63/?	X
20.02.44	R8971	439 Sqn	Benty Cowan. Ayr.	71/582090	S
18.03.44	JR439	440 Sqn	Loch Skerrow. Squadron move Ayr/Woodvale.	83/578668	M
27.03.45	MN532/	56 OTU	Stony Hill. Milfield.		
	FA-E			71/729215	M

HEINKEL He 111

09.08.40	–/	I/KG4	Eastmans Cairn. Operational sortie from Soesterberg,		
	5J+SH		Holland.	83/497673	S

JUNKERS Ju 88

25.03.43	144537/	II/KG6	Hare Hill. Probably cleared by 83 MU.		
	3E+HM		Aircraft from Deelen, Holland.	65/17-62-	X

LOCKHEED HUDSON

03.03.41	N7235	224 Sqn	Loch Bradan. Leuchars.	77/447963-	S
25 07.41	AE640	OADF	Feorlan, Mull of Kintyre.	68/639071	X

LOCKHEED NEPTUNE

10.10.56	WX545/C	36 Sqn	Mull of Kintyre. ASR exercise from Ballykelly.	68/597096	L

MILES MASTER

04.08.40	N7761	3 FPP	Burnhead. Ferrying Montrose/Reading.	77/06-14-	X

McDONNELL RF-4C PHANTOM

28.03.79	68-0566	1 TRS/	Cairnsmore. Cross-country from Alconbury.		
		10 TRW		83/495674-	S

NORTH AMERICAN HARVARD

16.01.53	FT401	22 FTS	Little Knock. Based at Syerston.	72/130263	M

NORTH AMERICAN MUSTANG

10.04.43	AG386	268 Sqn	Near Bargrennan. Nominal base Snailwell.	77/?	X

PERCIVAL PRENTICE

30.07.61	G-AOLR	–	Kilsyth Hills. Inbound to Renfrew.	64/682795	M

PERCIVAL PROCTOR

01.10.50	G-AMAL	–	Hundlashope Heights. Brough/Turnhouse.	72/247335	S

PIPER CHEROKEE

28.09.75	G-BATP	–	Bow Hill. Prestwick/Blackpool.	77/50-92-	X

REPUBLIC P-47 THUNDERBOLT

??.12.43		USAAF	Distinkhorn. Prestwick?	71/59-33-	

SUPERMARINE SEAFIRE

14.09.45	–	RCN?	Merrick. Allegedly from Anthorn.	77/42-85-	X
03.02.47	PR432	804 Sqn	Hill of Stake. Found by shepherd 09.04.47.		
			Donibristle/Eglinton.	63/274628	M

SUPERMARINE SPITFIRE

05.10.41	R7152	58 OTU	Pentland Hills. Cross-country from Grangemouth.	72/?	X
17.02.43	R6606	58 OTU	West Cairn Hill. Grangemouth.	72/11-58-	X

VICKERS VIKING

21.04.48	G-AIVE	BEA	Irish Law. On Beann Approach to Renfrew from Northolt.		
			All 20 on board escaped.	63/260593	M

Two civilian accidents. Above: **The remains of Proctor III G-AMAL near Peebles.**
Below: **The centre section, nacelles and one surviving Hercules engine from Viking G-AIVE near Largs.**

VICKERS WELLINGTON

25.01.41	R1164	20 OTU	Box Law. Ferrying Kirkbride/Lossiemouth.	63/256609	S
17.02.43	HX420	7 OTU	Sgreadan. On torpedo exercise from Machrihanish.	68/74-29-	S
27.02.43	HX779	7 OTU	Balnakeel Hill, Kintyre. Off course on flare-dropping exercise from Limavady.	68/?	X
02.12.43	LB137	6 OTU	Mull of Kintyre. Navex from Silloth.	68/?	X

Chapter Five

BORDER HILLS

As the chapter heading implies, this region straddles the border, although most of it is on the Scottish side. The Cheviot Hills are the dominant feature but there are many lesser heights which include the vast expanse of the Kielder Forest. Apart from the course of the Pennine Way, these hills are largely unfrequented by walkers and paths are few.

The wide valley of the Tweed was chosen for two aerodromes; Charter Hall and its satellite at Winfield. Night fighter crews were trained here on Beaufighters and Blenheims while, to the south of the Cheviots, their day fighter counterparts flew from Milfield, Brunton, Eshott and Acklington. Among the airfields built in the flat country around Carlisle were Crosby-on-Eden and Longtown which were used originally for day fighter training, then Coastal Command training on Beaufighters. There was an Elementary Flying Training School at Kingstown on the northern fringe of the city, at least two of its Tiger Moths being lost in high ground accidents.

The Halifax V on Glendhu Hill is quite an interesting wreck, although not as intact as we were once led to believe. The reader is reminded that permission is required from the Forestry Commission to visit the site. Most of the crew baled out when an engine caught fire.

The summit of The Cheviot is a large, flat, boggy area and happily the whole crew survived in two of the accidents up here. One involved a Stirling III whose salvage must have been something of an epic as there is very little left of such a large aircraft. The same can be said for the nearby Anson I which was carrying groundcrew and equipment during a squadron move. It was salvaged, repaired and flew again!

The most celebrated Cheviot wreck is the B-17G on Brayrdon Crag, which was taking part in a raid on Ulm in Germany. Over the North Sea the weather failed to clear as forecast and the bomber force was recalled to its bases. The Cheviot aircraft became disorientated because of misleading signals from German decoy transmitters and flew around for several hours trying to get a position fix. The B-17 failed to clear the mountain in driving snow and two of the crew were killed instantly. Two local shepherds were subsequently awarded the BEM for their part in the search for the survivors and the dog belonging to one of them received the Dickin Medal, the animal equivalent of the Victoria Cross.

The Lancaster X on Mid Hill was returning from a raid on the submarine pens at Bergen but wandered off course with fatal results for the entire crew. Another operational loss was the Hampden I which was homing to Waddington in Lincolnshire after a security patrol far out over the North Sea. The large remains of this aircraft are said to have been removed by helicopter about ten years ago but the RAF Museum have no knowledge of their preservation. Possibly they went to Otterburn to serve as targets on the ranges.

The Warwick ASR.VI on Cairn Hill was a surplus air-sea rescue aircraft which ironically was on its way to a MU for scrapping. Another unusual type this far north was a Mustang I which crashed on a training flight from Yorkshire. The Bewcastle Fells were the scene of several crashes, but the exact positions are unknown. Somewhere in this area a Hurricane I crashed in 1941, killing Prince Chirosakti of the Siamese royal family. A volunteer with the ATA, he was caught out by low cloud in a narrowing valley whilst ferrying the fighter from Kirkbride to Arbroath.

Simon Parry, author of *Intruders over Britain,* comments 'on the night of 24/25 March 1943, a total of eight Luftwaffe aircraft were lost on an extraordinary sortie over Northern Britain. Although some were credited to AA[anti-aircraft] units, it seems likely that many simply flew into high ground'. One was the Ju 88 on Linhope Rigg in the Cheviots, others included the Ju 88 on Hare Hill, south of Edinburgh and the Do 217 near Creetown, both being listed in the Southern Scotland section of this guide. The Do 217 on Madam Law was credited to AA fire.

ARMSTRONG WHITWORTH WHITLEY

15.10.40	P4952	10 Sqn	Watch Crags. Lost, short of fuel returning to Leeming from operations. Crew baled out.	80/788823	X

AVRO ANSON

05.03.40	N5094	49 Sqn	Cheviot. Force landing. Scampton/Kinloss.	81/851128	S

AVRO LANCASTER

03.03.44	DS650	1666 HCU	1½ miles east of Catcleugh Reservoir. Loss of control in cloud on navex from Wombleton.	80/77-03-	S
04.10.44	KB745/VR-V	419 Sqn	Mid Hill. Returning to Middleton St George from operations to Bergen.	74/919215	S

BOEING B-17G FORTRESS

16.12.44	44-6504	360th BS/303rd BG	Braydon Crag. Diverting to North Killingholme after aborted mission from Molesworth. Six survived.	74/895214	M

BOULTON PAUL DEFIANT

29.08.41	T4042	60 OTU	Hunt Law. Loss of control in cloud. East Fortune.	73/573577	
05.09.41	N1679	60 OTU	Edlingham Hill. Training flight from East Fortune.	81/956199	S

Below: **Pilot's grave marker, 60 OTU Defiant I T4042 on Hunt Law.**

BRISTOL BEAUFIGHTER

12.01.44	T5277	9 OTU	Bewcastle Fells. Practice controlled descent through cloud to Crosby-on-Eden	86/?	X
15.05.44	EL457	132 OTU	Hedgehope Hill. Night cross-country from East Fortune.	81/94-19-	X
18.11.44	T4772	9 OTU	Near Langholm. Crosby-on-Eden.	80/?	X

BRISTOL BLENHEIM

30.08.38	K7067	90 Sqn	Cottonshopehead. Navex from Bicester.	80/78-01-	X

DE HAVILLAND MOSQUITO

12.12.44	DD753	54 OTU	The Curr. On night exercise from Charter Hall.	74/850235	M

DE HAVILLAND TIGER MOTH

01.03.43	N9462	15 EFTS	The Carts Kingstown.	87/836730	S
04.11.44	T6828	15 EFTS	Glen Dhu. Kingstown.	80/560853-	X

DORNIER Do217E-4

25.03.43	5432/ US+DL	3/KG2	Madam Law. Shot down during raid on Edinburgh.	74/865268	S

HANDLEY PAGE HALIFAX

15.10.44	DK116/ GG-Z	1667 HCU	Glendhu Hill. Engine fire, some of the crew baled out. Sandtoft.	80/580862	L
17.02.45	NR126/ PT-X	420 Sqn	Shill Moor. Returning to Tholthorpe, but diverted to Winfield, following ops to Wesel	80/945113	S

HANDLEY PAGE HAMPDEN

18.03.40	L4063	50 Sqn	Windy Gyle. Large sections removed possibly to Otterburn Ranges. Returning to Waddington from security patrol.	80/847158	S

HAWKER HART

10.10.39	K6482	152 Sqn	Cheviot. Turnhouse/Acklington.	74/919221	

HAWKER HURRICANE

13.10.41	Z2349	3 Del Flt	Near Newcastlelon. On ferry flight.	86/?	X
03.11.41	Z3150/ FT-V	43 Sqn	Peel Fell. Acklington.	80/62-00-	X
16.03.42	P3902	59 OTU	Haggy Hill. Crosby-on-Eden.	79/28-85-	X
26.02.43	P8813	55 OTU	Bewcastle Fells. Annan.	86/?	X

HAWKER SEA HURRICANE

19.08.44	BW855	731 Sqn	Hepple Whitefield. Sealand/Easthaven.	81/98-99-	X

JUNKERS Ju88

25.03.43	144354 3E+BH	I/KG6	Linhope Rigg. From Deelen, Holland.	80/945169	S

MILES MASTER

29.09.41	W8594	59 OTU	Tarnbeck Fell, Liddesdale. Crosby-on-Eden.	86/?	X

NORTH AMERICAN MUSTANG

19.02.43	AG617	4 Sqn	Troughend Common. Navex from Clifton.	80/85-91-	X

PIPER CHEROKEE

13.02.79	G-BHDG		Hedgehope Hill. Edinburgh/Usworth.	81/94-19-	X

SHORT STIRLING

25.09.44	EE972	1665 HCU	Cheviot. Navex from Tilstock.	81/915200	S

SUPERMARINE SPITFIRE

25.03.43	P8587	57 OTU	Bellyside Hill. Eshott.Cleared	74/906225	S

VICKERS WELLINGTON

30.10.40	T2546	99 Sqn	Near Otterburn. Lost returning to Newmarket from . ops to Berlins.	80/?	X
15.01.42	Z1078	150 Sqn	West Hill, Cheviot. Returning to Snaith. from ops to Hamburg	74/893223	M
01.03.43	R3173	15 OTU	Blackburn Fell. Dived into ground from cloud. Navex from Harwell.	80/80-93-	X
28.10.45	LP665/C	105 OTU	Edges Green. Navex from Bramcote.	80/718687	S

VICKERS WARWICK

23.07.46	HG136	269 Sqn	Cairn Hill.Thornaby/Brackla.	80/900195	L

Chapter Six

WESTERN PENNINES

Ranging from the high mountains of the north, such as Cross Fell and the Howgills, to the moorland of Lancashire, this region is far less popular with walkers than the Lake District or the Yorkshire Moors. Would-be investigators are warned that the hills in the north are extremely rough and pathless, which makes wreck hunting even more arduous than usual. This loneliness, however, is an added attraction. The moors further south are not so high or extensive, but in bad weather they can be just as hazardous to the inexperienced or ill-equipped.

Apart from those around Carlisle and the Solway Firth described in the Southern Scotland section, there were few other aerodromes on the fringes of this area of high ground. It was, however, criss-crossed with long distance navigation training routes and the so-called Barnard Castle Gap was often used by ATA ferry pilots who were not supposed to fly in or above cloud. Attempts to make it over the Pennines under a lowering cloud base brought death to several of them.

The best-known victim of a navex which went wrong was the Stirling III on Mickle Fell, from which only the tail gunner survived. This wreck was one of the most intact in Britain until its recovery in 1980, but there is still quite a lot of wreckage overlooked or ignored at the time. A Mosquito B.35 crashed on Mickle Fell whilst engaged rather mysteriously in 'Cosmic Ray research' but I have not been able to locate its position.

Surprisingly little remains of the accidents on Cross Fell's large and lonely summit plateau and the salvage teams must have expended great efforts in recovering them.

The Spitfire I on High Scald Fell a few miles away was the first of many lost to high ground during the type's service career. Another fighter, the Tomahawk I on Red Gill Moss, was one of the initial batch for the RAF which in the panic after Pearl Harbor was taken over by the USAAF and then subsequently released to the British. It was on an army co-operation exercise when it crashed. 'Castle Moss' where a Botha from Millom crashed in 1941 is not shown on the one inch OS Map but it is believed to be south of the Tomahawk site by a few miles. Another mystery is the origin of the P-47 fragments on Pendle Hill. It could have come from Burtonwood, Warton or the training base at Atcham, near Shrewsbury.

The Halifax II on Hoarside Moor had got lost on the way back from mine-laying near the Friesian Islands, but fortunately most of the crew survived. A memorial stone records the names of the crew of a Wellington IC on Anglezarke Moor. The pilot was thought to have lost control, possibly due to severe icing, and the aircraft sustained structural damage in the resulting high speed dive.

Several USAAF aircraft crashed in the south of the area, with three concentrated within a mile in the Trough of Bowland. The B-24J Liberator was on a training flight from Norfolk and must have been a combat veteran as it was described in USAAF terminology as 'war weary'. Close by, but two years before, a pair of P-38G Lightnings had flown into the hillside in cloud whilst on a practice flight from Goxhill on the south bank of the Humber. They belonged to the 78th Fighter Group which, when re-equipped with Thunderbolts, was to achieve a remarkable reputation flying escort missions from Duxford.

There are several other wrecks around the picturesque Trough of Bowland, but much of the moorland is private so it is essential to request permission to visit the sites. The Douglas C-54G was a Berlin Airlift aircraft and was en route to Burtonwood for overhaul when it wandered off course. A propeller blade was the largest part left on the fell but I believe this has now gone.

Winter Hill is reasonably close to roads and it seems certain that little or nothing is to be seen at the crash sites up here. It is known, for example, that Bristol B.170 Wayfarer G-AICS was recovered in 1958 after a crash which killed 35 people. A Chipmunk T.10 from Woodvale flew into the hill in cloud in the 1960s and, although it finished up on its back, both occupants were able to extricate themselves and the aircraft was later removed.

AIRSPEED OXFORD

| 24.12.43 | BM837 | 410 Sqn | Winter Hill. Acklington. | | 109/66-15- | X |

ARMSTRONG WHITWORTH WHITLEY

| 01.05.40 | K9039 | 51 Sqn | Burnside Fell. Crash-landing short of fuel. Dishforth. Returning from a raid on Fornebu, Norway. | 103/67-53- | S |
| 30.10.40 | P4957 | 10 Sqn | Near Slaggyford. Returning to Leeming from ops. | 86/? | S |

AVRO ANSON

07.01.42	R3409	1 AOS	Brant Fell. Navex from Wigtown Aircraft iced up, crew baled out.	89/67-96-	M
18.03.43	DJ453	4 AOS	Cross Fell. Navex from West Freugh. Aircraft iced up in cloud. All crew survived.	91/699345	S
09.02.44	N4919	2 OAFU	Wolfhole Crag. Navex from Millom. Iced up and crash landed. All crew survived.	103/63-58-	M
08.01.45	EF935	1 OAFU	Langdale Fell. Navex from Wigtown.	89/65-00-	

Below: **Anson I DJ453 on Cross Fell with a salvage gang from No.83 Maintenance Unit, Woolsington.** Peter Dobson via D W Earl

AVRO TUTOR

15.01.40	K3422	500 Sqn	Greenhill. Lost in fog, pilot baled out. Ferrying Linton-on-Ouse/Kirkbride.	86/650508	M

BELL AIRACOBRA

22.11.42	BX195	1st FG	Near Scalebar Force. Goxhill.	98/?	S

BLACKBURN BOTHA

22.08.41	L6416	2 AOS	Castle Moss. Encountered bad weather on last leg of cross-country from Millom.	92/?	X

BLACKBURN SKUA

12.09.40	'L2929'	4 FPP	Near High Bentham. Engine failure on ferry flight. Hullavington/Donibristle. Pilot baled out.	92/2	S

BOULTON PAUL DEFIANT

18.08.41	N1651/ JT-Z	256 Sqn	Marshaw Fell. On training flight from Squires Gate.	102/60-52-	S

BRISTOL BEAUFIGHTER

04.07.43	JM223	9 OTU	Croglin Fell. On practice controlled descent through cloud. Crosby-on-Eden.	86/60-49-	X

BRISTOL BLENHEIM

26.10.38	L1252/H	34 Sqn	Wemmergill Moor. Catterick/Kingstown		M
26.11.40	R3914/ YH-N	21 Sqn	Near Middleton-in-Teesdale. Lost returning from operational flight		X
09.08.44	BA246/14	12 PAFU	Bleasdale. Training flight from Woodvale.	102/582483	M

CONSOLIDATED B-24J LIBERATOR

02.01.45	42-100322 715th BS/448th BG		Burn Fell. Seething/Warton.	103/672533	M
19.02.45	42-50668	491st BG	Hameldon Black. North Pickenham/Warton.	103/913306	M

CURTISS TOMAHAWK

10.02.43	AH744	1472 Flt	Red Gill Moss. Army co-op exercise from Catterick.	92/876158	M

DE HAVILLAND DRAGON RAPIDE

20.06.39	G-AERE	–	Langdon Common. Heston/Newcastle.	92/892321	S

DE HAVILLAND DH 60 MOTH

21.04.36	G-AARE	–	Cross Fell. Engine only. Doncaster/Kingstown.	91/685344	

DE HAVILLAND MOSQUITO

05.01.50	VP199	109 Sqn	Mickle Fell area. Missing for some time. Coningsby.	92/?	X

DE HAVILLAND TIGER MOTH

27.01.43	T5679	15 EFTS	Six miles south west of Alston. Kingstown.	86/?	X

DE HAVILLAND VENOM

04.03.57	WR557	22 MU	Croglin Fell. On test from Silloth.	86/640471	L

Above: **Massive undercarriage leg from B-24J Liberator 42-50668 on Hameldon Hill.** D W Earl

Below: **Memorial to the nine aircrew who perished on board Halifax II BB310 on Great Dun Fell.**
David E Thompson

DOUGLAS C-54 SKYMASTER

| 07.01.49 | 45-543 | USAF | Stake House Fell. Berlin Airlift aircraft returning to Burtonwood for maintenance. | 102/556497 | S |

DOUGLAS DAKOTA

| 10.01.46 | KG502/A1383 TCU | | Cold Fell. Night cross-country from Crosby-on-Eden. | 86/588563 | S |
| 17.10.61 | G-AMVC | BKS | Croglin Fell. Woolsington/Crosby-on-Eden. | 86/599506 | S |

FAIRCHILD UC-61 FORWARDER

| 07.08.42 | '41-54885' | 5 ADG | Winter Hill. Believed cleared. | 109/66-15- | X |

GLOSTER METEOR

| 24.03.54 | WD778 | 228 OCU | Dufton Fell. Leeming/Acklington. | 91/723295 | L |

HANDLEY PAGE HALIFAX

21.01.43	DT581	51 Sqn	Hoarside Moor. Returning to Snaith from mine-laying off Friesian Islands.	103/935298	L
12.04.44	BB310	1674 HCU	Great Dun Fell. Navex from Longtown	91/697324	S
26.08.44	MZ658	431 Sqn	Allenheads. Mainly buried. Out of fuel, ex-ops. Crew baled out. Croft.	87/838506	S

HANDLEY PAGE HAMPDEN

| 16.08.42 | P4318 | 14 OTU | Arkengarthdale Moor. Navex from Cottesmore. | 92/94-06- | |

HAWKER HURRICANE

26.04.41	V7619	55 OTU	Allendale, Usworth.	87/?	X
06.06.41	V6962	55 OTU	Langdon Common. Usworth.	92/883327	X
18.07.41	V7534	59 OTU	Dufton Fell. Lost in bad visibility. Crosby-on-Eden.	91/73-28-	X
11.11.41	P3318	55 OTU	Waskerley Park Reservoir. Usworth.	92/02-44-	S
28.04.43	P3901	55 OTU	Scarrowmanwick Fell. Annan.	86/61-47-	X

LOCKHEED HUDSON

| 06.09.42 | N7325/B59 | 1 OTU | Wildboar Scar. Silloth. | 91/688329 | S |

LOCKHEED P-38G LIGHTNING

| 26.01.43 | 42-12905 | 83thFS/ | Dunsop Fell. Training flight from Goxhill. | 103/674541 | S |
| | 42-12928 | 78th FG | | | |

McDONNELL PHANTOM

| 21.11.72 | XV477/C | 6 Sqn | Thack Moor. Ran into cloud on low-level cross-country from Coningsby. | 91/613461 | S |

MILES MASTER

| 19.12.41 | W8479 | TFPP | Arant Haw Fell. Shawbury/Kirkbride. | 89/662946 | S |
| 28.01.42 | T8614 | 4 FPP | Beldoo Hill. Dumfries/Catterick. | 92/885136 | S |

NORTH AMERICAN MUSTANG

| 29.11.42 | AP208 | 4 Sqn | Holdron Moss. Cross-country from York. | 103/609509 | S |
| 04.06.44 | 43-6565 | 496th FTG | Near Rochdale. Goxhill. | 109/? | X |

| 17.08.44 | AG443 | 41 OTU | Near Clitheroe. Hawarden. | 109/? | X |
| 29.07.45 | SR411 | 316 Sqn | Darwen Moor. Coltishall | 109/692191 | S |

REPUBLIC P-47 THUNDERBOLT

| – | – | USAAF | Pendle Hill. From Burtonwood? | 103/80-42- | S |

SHORT STIRLING

| 19.10.44 | LK488/ | 1651 HCU | Mickle Fell. Mostly recovered for RAF Museum,but later scrapped. | | |
| | QQ-E | | Night navex from Wratting Common. | 92/812248 | S |

SUPERMARINE SPITFIRE

18.07.39	K9888	41 Sqn	High Scald Fell. Catterick/Kingstown.	91/708313	S
14.05.41	P8161	9 MU	Near Colne. Ferrying from Cosford.	103/?	X
27.03.42	P8463	81 Sqn	Near Stanhope. Lost formation in cloud. Turnhouse.	92/?	X
16.07.42	W3628	315 Sqn	Wolfhole Crag. Woodvale.	103/63-58-	S
28.12.42	AD230	317 Sqn	White Moss Fell. Woodvale.	102/58-50	

VICKERS WELLINGTON

20.08.42	T2715/	25 OTU	Meldon Hill, Dufton Fell. Navex from Finningley.		
	PP-E			81/73-28-	X
16.11.43	Z8799	28 OTU	Anglezarke Moor. On Bullseye Exercise, lost control in cloud, possibly due to icing. Wymeswold. Memorial nearby	109/628167	S

Left: **Memorial to the crew of 25 OTU Wellington IC Z8799 on Anglezarke Moor.** B G Barlow

Two views of the salvage operation of the Mickle Fell Stirling III LK488, a 'combined operation' between the RAF an members of the Air Training Corps. The substantial wreck was airlifted off using a Puma HC.1. Sadly, the decision was later taken to scrap all the remains. Both Ken Ellis collection

Chapter Seven

YORKSHIRE MOORS & DALES

Many bomber aerodromes were built in the Vale of York because of operational considerations, despite the high ground to the north, north east and west. A small error of navigation while letting down at night, perhaps with flak damage and low on fuel, could be fatal. Most of the accidents on the moors thus involved bomber aircraft: Whitleys and Wellingtons in the early years of the war, later on, Halifaxes and Lancasters.

The network of roads and tracks over much of the moorland enabled crashed aircraft to be removed with relative ease, although parts were frequently buried on site. The more interesting wrecks therefore tend to be on the higher mountains on the eastern flank of the Pennines. These include Great Whernside and an entirely different summit 20 miles away confusingly known also as Whernside. Thanks are due to David Thompson of Stockton-on-Tees for his help in expanding the previous list for this area.

The two Dornier Do217Es on 17th December 1942 were taking part in an intruder raid and ran into bad weather. The one on Wheeldale Moor was hit by AA fire after crossing the coast and apparently crashed whilst trying to land on the rough ground. The Junkers Ju88 on Eston Moor was engaged in a reconnaissance mission to Manchester when it was shot down by a Spitfire V of No.41 Squadron, based at Catterick.

The largest group of sites is to be found on Great Whernside, but there is not much left owing to wartime salvage operations and subsequent amateur efforts. No.60 MU recovered most of the B-17G with the aid of a horse and sledge and were responsible also for clearing much of the widely-scattered Halifax II wreckage. In July 1980, a local scout group carried a propeller down from the B-17 and it is now on display in Kettlewell where there is a memorial to the airmen killed on the mountain.

Some miles north of Great Whernside is Buckden Pike where a Wellington IC on a night cross-country flight crashed in January 1942. The crew were all Polish and the rear gunner, the sole survivor, later raised a memorial on the summit to his comrades. Another rear gunner escaped almost unhurt when a Wellington III flew into Whernside. A few hundred yards away a Barracuda II did the same thing just after the war, the pilot being lucky enough to walk away. Large parts of this aircraft were recovered for a now defunct air museum at York and their ultimate fate is unknown.

Several Whitleys collided with the moors whilst returning from operations, three the same night on one occasion. The soft peaty ground was relatively yielding and happily many of the crews survived. The long trips in slow aircraft with minimal navigation aids took a heavy toll and one of the crashes occurred after a pilot fell asleep at the controls from sheer fatigue. Fortunately, he lived to tell the tale.

On Arden Great Moor, a Spitfire XVI, was returning home after taking part in Acklington's Battle of Britain display in September 1945 when it crashed in bad weather. The remains once included an almost intact wing, but the site was apparently cleared within the last ten years for reasons unknown. Perhaps it was reported by overflying aircraft? The Whitley V in the same area had previously been abandoned by its crew when they ran out of fuel trying to find RAF Leeming after a raid on Stettin, a target which was at about the limit of this aircraft's range.

AIRSPEED ENVOY
15.02.35	G-ADBZ	–	Hutton Moor. Dales. North Eastern Airways	X

AIRSPEED OXFORD
29.08.43	DF471	427 Sqn	Great Caum. Leeming/?	98/702828 S
08.01.45	LW903	18 PAFU	Urra Moor.Transit flight Church Lawford/?	100/598012 S

ARMSTRONG WHITWORTH WHITLEY
15.10.40	T4143/ ZA-J	10 Sqn	Arden Great Moor. Returning to Leeming from ops, Stettin, out of fuel, crew baled out.	100/497935 S
21.10.40	T4171/ GE-O	58 Sqn	Greenhow Moor. Returning to Linton-on-Ouse from ops.	93/598022 S
23.08.41	T4234	10 Sqn	Widdale Fell. Returning to Leeming from ops.	98/804883 S
11.12.41	Z9188	10 Sqn	Eavestones. Dales. Returning Dishforth from ops Cologne.	X
28.03.42	Z9221	77 Sqn	Kirkby Malzard Moor. Bad weather forced early return to Leeming on ops.	99/17-75- X
28.03.42	Z9481	51 Sqn	Great Whernside. Returning to Dishforth, ex-ops to St Nazaire.	98/005716 S
28.03.42	Z9274/ MH-U	51 Sqn	Horncliffe Well. Returning to Dishforth ex-ops to St Nazaire.	104/129434 S

AVRO LANCASTER
14.10.42	W4233	61 Sqn	Hagg House Moor. Returning to Syerston ex-ops to Kiel.	93/439995 S
30.01.43	ED481	9 Sqn	Hawnby Hill. Waddington.	S
17.12.43	DS737/ EQ-C	408 Sqn	Murton Common. Believed cleared. Returning to Linton-on-Ouse ex-ops Berlin.	100/512882
16.05.44	KB701	419 Sqn	Helmsley Moor. Navex from Middleton St George.	93/586928 S
18.10.44	NF961	630 Sqn	Far Moor. Cross-country from East Kirkby.	100/493995 S
05.11.45	RA571/ AL-D	429 Sqn	Beamsley Beacon. Airtest from Leeming.	104/101523 S

BOEING B-17G FORTRESS
17.05.45	44-8683	388th BG	Great Whernside. Navex from Knettishall.	98/003728 S

BRISTOL BEAUFIGHTER
20.01.43	T5299	2 OTU	Near Huntersworth. Navex from Catfoss.	94/67-02- X
28.04.43	R2152	2 OTU	Waites Moor. Night navex from Catfoss.	94/658034 S

BRISTOL BLENHEIM
21.03.40	L1117	219 Sqn	Kirbymoorside. Catterick.	94/61-00- X
18.07.41	L1449	54 OTU	Bransdale. Night Flying from Church Fenton.	94/604998 S
??.02.42	–	54 OTU	Todd Intake Moor. Church Fenton.	93/599996 S

Right: **Scant remains of Lancaster III ED481 'WS-N' of 9 Squadron with Hawnby Hill in the background. Returning from a raid on Hamburg it was diverted from its base at Waddington to Leeming, with fatal consequences for its mixed RAF and RCAF crew.** David E Thompson

Above: **Water-filled crater and scattered wreckage – sad testament to the last moments of 54 OTU Mosquito NF.30 NT266 on Pockley Moor.** David E Thompson

DE HAVILLAND MOSQUITO

02.03.43	DD450	25 Sqn	White Crag. Holding for approach to Church Fenton.	104/068466	S
08.11.46	NT266	54 OTU	Pockley Moor. Loss of control in cloud. Leeming.	94/620925	M
13.12.48	RL197	228 OCU	Great Whernside Training flight from Leeming.	98/000734	S

DE HAVILLAND TIGER MOTH

06.09.45	N6793	4 EFTS	Spaunton Moor, Cross-country from Brough.	94/72-93-	S

DORNIER Do 217E-4

17.12.42	4342/ U5+GR	7/KG2	Crow Nest. Raid on York from Deelen, Holland.	93/553914	S
17.12.42	4348/ U5+AK	2/KG2	Wheeldale Moor. Raid on York from Deelen, Holland.	94/789984	S

FAIREY BARRACUDA

15.12.45	DR306	769 Sqn	Whernside. Based at Rattray, Pilot unhurt	98/743802	M

GLOSTER JAVELIN

29.09.59	XA662/N	228 OCU	Apedale. Leeming.	98/017941	M

HANDLEY PAGE HALIFAX

12.07.43	DG404	1663 HCU	Heathfield Moor. Navex from Rufforth.	99/11-67-	S
23.11.43	DT578	1658 HCU	Great Whernside. Navex from Riccall.	98/001730	S
31.01.44	DK185	1664 HCU	Black Beck Hole, On navex from Dishforth	104/093467	S
18.03.44	LL178	434 Sqn	Near Arden Hall. Croft.	100/505912	S

28.01.45	LL576	1664 HCU	Three miles north west of Pateley Bridge.		
			One engine failed on navex from Dishforth.	99/?	X
?	–	–	Slipstone Crags.	99/138820	S

HAWKER HURRICANE

22.04.40	L2009	11 Gp Pool	Six miles west of Ripon. Ferrying.	99/?	X
10.01.41	P3522	213 Sqn	Caldbergh Moor.Leconfield.	99/10-83-	X
19.05.41	P3772	55 OTU	Lockton Low Moor. Usworth.	94/850923	S
14.06.41	V7024	55 OTU	Redshaw Moss. Usworth.	98/81-84-	X
12.06.42	AG680	5 FPP	Near West Keld. Ferrying Henlow/Silloth		X

JUNKERS Ju 88A

| 30.03.41 | 0115/ | 1F/123 | Eston Moor. Reconnaissance to Manchester, | | |
| | 4U+GH | | shot down by a Spitfire V from 41 Squadron. | 93/566171 | S |

LOCKHEED HUDSON

| 11.02.40 | N7294 | 220 Sqn | Warren Moor.Thornaby. | 94/616083 | S |
| 22.01.41 | T9371 | 220 Sqn | Near Ingleby Arncliffe. Thornaby. | 100/? | X |

NORTH AMERICAN MUSTANG

| 15.12.42 | AG586 | 613 Sqn | Nr Pateley Bridge, Pilot baled out in bad weather. Ouston. | 99/? | S |

PIPER CHEROKEE

| 23.09.69 | G-AVYN | – | Ashfoldgill Gill Head. | 99/078683 | M |

Below: **Dave Earl with the surprising amount of Cherokee 180D G-AVYN at Ashfold Gill Head.** Dave Earl

SHORT STIRLING

| 14.08.44 | EE975/
GP-O | 1660 HCU | Old Cote Moor. Engine failure at night, unable to
maintain height. Most of crew baled out. | 98/927728 | S |

SUPERMARINE SPITFIRE

| 25.01.42 | AD545 | 122 Sqn | Spaunton Moor. Scorton. | 94/? | X |
| 16.09.45 | SM278/
I4-F | 567Sqn | Arden Great Moor. Acklington/Manston. | 100/483935 | S |

VICKERS WARWICK

| 13.11.43 | BV336/
MF-P | 280 Sqn | Smeaton Low Moor. Thornaby. | 94/895045 | S |

VICKERS WELLINGTON

16.01.42	W5493	104 Sqn	Arden Great Moor. Returning to Driffield from ops to Emden.	100/495934	S
31.01.42	N2848/G	18 OTU	Buckden Pike. Navex from Bramcote. Memorial on site.	98/962779	S
03.09.42	Z8808	11 OTU	Ashfold Gill Beck. Aircraft almost uncontrollable in bad weather. Crew survived. Bassingbourn.	99/077687	S
03.09.42	DV718	11 OTU	Blake Hill. Navex from Bassingbourn. Some wreckage recovered by South Yorks Air Museum.	98/024733	M
12.02.43	BJ778/ ZL-A	427 Sqn	Black Intake Moor. Returning to Croft from ops.	100/581997	M
21.04.44	BK347	30 OTU	Whernside. Off track on navex from Hixon.	98/743817	S
28.05.45	HE226	17 OTU	Bycliffe. On navex from Silverstone.	98/013687	S
–	–		Brayshaw Scar.	98/925726	S

WESTLAND LYSANDER

| 14.01.41 | T1689 | 4 Sqn | Ilkley Moor. Lost in bad weather on ferry flight to
or from Clifton. | 104/11-46- | X |

Chapter Eight

LAKE DISTRICT

On the coastal plain to the north west of the Lakeland Fells lay the MU airfields of Silloth and Kirkbride, the former in its early years doubling as a Coastal Command Hudson OTU. In the south there were three training aerodromes; an Air Gunners School at Barrow, an Observer School at Millom and at Cark an organisation for teaching instructional techniques, the Staff Pilot Training Unit. Aircraft from the Observer Schools at Dumfries and Wigtown frequently overflew the area, as did Wellingtons from the Bomber OTUs in the Midlands.

It will come as no surprise to learn that Ansons were the most common casualties on the fells, at least 13 being lost here. On a terrible night of thunderstorms in August 1943, No.10 (O)AFU at Dumfries lost no less than three of them. The next morning found search aircraft combing the Irish Sea for survivors. The wrecks were discovered eventually on the fells, a few of the crewmen having survived.

The remains of three veteran biplanes can still be seen, the earliest being the Vildebeeste III and Hind which crashed in June 1937 and the Hawker Hector as late as 1941. The latter was being ferried to the MU at Dumfries when the engine failed, the pilot being killed in an attempt to crash-land amongst the rocks of Red Pike. The occupants of the DH.86 biplane airliner which force-landed on Bolton Ground were fortunate to escape serious injury.

Pieces of an Avenger II are still embedded in Great Gully above Wastwater, but the battered engine which lay on the lake shore now seems to have gone. There has been much 'tidying up' by the National Park authorities in recent years and wreckage at some sites near popular walking routes has been buried or removed.

Perhaps the most interesting site is on Great Carrs where a Halifax V hit the summit and was later pushed over the cliffs into Broad Slack by the salvage crew. Much of its remains lie here to this day and most walkers are familiar with this wreck, although few are aware of the story behind it and generally assume that it is a Lancaster. The circumstances are yet another minor tragedy of the Second World War, all seven crew being killed in the accident. Completely lost on a night cross-country through inexperience, the pilot descended below safety height hoping to break cloud and pinpoint his position.

On two separate occasions, pairs of Hurricanes from No.55 OTU hit high ground in formation. There is little left of any of them, most of the wreckage of those on Slight Side being covered by rocks. In March 1941, two Hurricanes from No.601 Squadron on a transit flight were also lost after becoming separated in a snowstorm. Another fighter, this time a Spitfire XVI, went missing on 20th November 1947 and was found by a shepherd on Scafell on 1st May of the following year.

An unusual aircraft was the US Navy Douglas AD-4B Skyraider on Banna Fell. The crew escaped serious injury and the wreckage was later buried. Some years later, a Canadian Sabre hit Iron Crag, leaving a long trail of debris. The fin with squadron badge is now in the RAF Millom Museum. Another post-war crash involved a USAF Beech Expeditor light transport which ran into a blizzard. Both occupants struggled down the fell after a cold night sheltering in the fuselage.

A perennial mystery no nearer to solution is the identity of an aircraft which crashed on the Old Man of Coniston on 14th October 1942. The records of RAF Millom say it was a 'Lockheed aircraft', whilst those of RAF Ayr, from which it departed, quote it as a 'Beechcraft Twin'. It was being flown from Ayr to Limavady in Northern Ireland by two American civilian ferry pilots employed by the Lockheed Corporation. It may have been a Beech C-45, the type later to be known as the Expeditor.

The Cumbrian Fells are very steep and craggy and particularly dangerous in mist, although on the credit side there are plenty of well-worn paths. The famous series of guides to the Lake District written by A W Wainwright are a recommended source of information on routes, a few of the wrecks being mentioned. The Oxford on Caw Fell, for example, is described picturesquely in his inimitable fashion as 'ruins of aeroplane'!

AIRSPEED OXFORD

02.11.41	AT486	2 AOS	Caw Fell. Navex from Millom.	89/131106	M

AVRO ANSON

20.09.42	N4B69/60	20 AFU	Muncaster Fell. Navex from Millom.	96/12-99-	X
01.10.42	DJ410	4 AOS	Green Gable. Four of crew survived. Navex from West Freugh.	90/213107	S
01.01.43	AX145/31	1 OAFU	Frozen Fell. Navex from Wigtown.	90/287335	S
01.01.43	W2629	1 OAFU	High Pike. All crew survived. Night navex from Wigtown.	90/32-35-	X
14.02.43	DJ466/BP	10 OAFU	Grisedale Pike . Navex from Dumfries.	90/198236	S
08.04.43	EG361/D3	5 AOS	Lords Seat. Navex from Jurby	90/204266	S
09.08.43	DJ222/A2	10 OAFU	Green Gable. Night navex from Dumfries.	90/215107	S
09.08.43	N5053/ G2	10 OAFU	Great Dod. Night navex from Dumfries. Four of the crew survived.	90/344205	S
09.08.43	DJ275/AL	10 OAFU	Sca Fell. Night navex from Dumfries.	90/209061	S
30.01.44	MG393/ Y3	AN&BS	Starling Dod.Night navex from Jurby. Descended through cloud when fuel almost exhausted.	89/144157	S
20.03.44	EG686/90	SPTU	Swirl How. Navex from Cark.	90/278002	M
17.11.44	MG464/J	AN&BS	Grisedale Pike. Navex from Jurby. Caught in downdraught.	90/197219	S
02.01.45	LT741/5	10 AGS	Black Combe. Apparently entered cloud on gunnery exercise from Barrow.	96/140859	S

BEECH C-45 EXPEDITOR

12.03.47	–	USAF	Black Combe. Crew escaped. Prestwick/Bovingdon.	96/131856	M

BOEING B-17E

14.09.43	41-9051	482nd BG	Skiddaw. Training flight from Alconbury.	90/258286	S

BRISTOL BEAUFIGHTER

15.11.43	EL285/E	9 OTU	Wolf Crag. Night flying from Crosby-on-Eden.	90/353223	S

CESSNA 150E

22.02.66	G-ASYH	–	Black Combe. Blackpool/Newcastle.	90/13-85-	S

DE HAVILLAND DOMINIE
30.08.46   X7394   782 Sqn   Broad Crag. Abbotsinch/Stretton.   89/218078 M

DE HAVILLAND MOSQUITO
10.04.45   HK141   51 OTU   Catstye Carn. Night navex from Cranfield.   90/346151 S

DE HAVILLAND DH.86B
28.07.39   L7596   24 Sqn   Bolton Ground. Hendon/Sydenham. Forced-landing.   96/24-83-   X

DOUGLAS SKYRAIDER
02.10.53   132370 USS *Wasp*   Banna Fell. Mainly buried. USS *Wasp* (in Irish Sea)/Prestwick.
Crew survived.   89/106174 S

ENGLISH ELECTRIC CANBERRA
20.01.58   WT505   58 Sqn   Ponsonby Fell. Site virtually cleared. Wyton.   89/085070 S

GENERAL DYNAMICS F-111E
05.03.75   68-0081   20 TFW   Ulthwaite Rig. Upper Heyford.   90/518094 S

GRUMMAN AVENGER
16.01.45   JZ390   763 Sqn   Great Gully, Wastwater. Engine now in lake.
On night navex from Inskip.   89/148038 S

HANDLEY PAGE HALIFAX
24.01 44   JP182   14 FPP   Eel Crag. Kinloss/Kemble.   90/193204 S
22.10.44   LL505/ 1659 HCU   Great Carrs. Became completely lost on navex
        FD-S   from Topcliffe.   90/272008 L

Below: **Halifax undercarriage parts and memorial cross on the summit of great Carrs.** Dave Earl

HAWKER HECTOR

| 08.09.41 | K8096 | 1 SAC | Red Pike. Ferrying Binbrook/Dumfries. | 89/168105 | M |

HAWKER HIND

| 05.06.37 | K6614 | 98 Sqn | Thornthwaite. West Freugh/Hucknall. | 90/428106 | M |

HAWKER HURRICANE

31.03.41	V7539	601 Sqn	Scar Crags. Flying with V6987 from Northolt to Crosby-on-Eden. Got lost in blizzard.	90/213205	M
31.03.41	V6987/ UF-L	601 Sqn	Birk House Moor. Northolt/Crosby-on-Eden.	90/366170	S
12.08.41	V6565/ V7742	55 OTU	Slight Side. Operational training from Usworth.	90/211049	M
20.07.42	R4217	55 OTU	Dowthwaitehead. Cross-country from Usworth.	90/37-21-	X
21.01.43	AF959	55 OTU	Great Calva. Cross-country from Annan.	90/286316	X
23.04.43	AG264 and AG275	55 OTU	Brim Fell. Much of one of the aircraft is in Low Water. Annan.	97/275994 97/273991	S S

LOCKHEED HUDSON

| 10.11.42 | AM680 | 1 OTU | Beda Head. Mainly buried. Navex from Silloth | 90/427171 | S |

MILES HAWK TRAINER

| 22.09.52 | G-ALGJ | – | Lank Rigg. | 89/088123 | S |

NORTH AMERICAN F-86 SABRE

| 26.06.59 | 23380/ BB-380 | 421 Sqn/ RCAF | Iron Crag. Prestwick/Wethersfield. | 89/121120 | M |

PIPER CHEROKEE

| 17.09.66 | G-ASEK | – | Esk Hause. Milfield/Newcastle. | 89/23-08- | S |

PIPER CHEROKEE ARROW

| 13.2.91 | G-IPJC | – | Skiddaw. Stapleford/? | 90/- | |

PIPER SARATOGA

| 29.11.87 | G -BNYS | – | Bow Fell. Staverton/Prestwick. | 89/24-06- | X |

SUPERMARINE SPITFIRE

| 20.11.47 | SL611 | 603 Sqn | Sca Fell. Wreckage found by shepherd. 01.05.48. Hawarden/Turnhouse. | 89/21-07- | X |

VICKERS VILDEBEESTE

| 04.06.37 | K4607 | 42 Sqn | Crinkle Crags. Filton/Donibristle. | 89/254053 | S |

VICKERS WELLINGTON

08.02.42	T2714/ DD-C	220TU	Burn Tod. Crashed after radio failure on navex from Wellesbourne Mountford.	90/287330	S
16.12.42	X3336	23 OTU	Carlside. 48 miles off track on night navex from Pershore.	90/246288	S
16.06.44	HZ715	22 OTU	Red Pike. Navex from Wellesbourne Mountford.	90/159156	X

Chapter Nine

ISLE OF MAN

Manx wreck sites consist mainly of approximate locations gleaned from official records. I and a few other people have found several of the sites and the map references are given where known. As the island's hills are neither very high nor extensive, it was a relatively easy task to recover the debris. Much of it found its way to a dump at RAF Jurby. It seems certain that there are at least a few fragments to be found at most sites.

Apart from Jurby which housed an air navigation and bombing school, there were two other Manx wartime aerodromes. Andreas was built as a fighter base but with the Luftwaffe rarely seen over the Irish Sea after 1941, it was downgraded to an air gunners school. Ronaldsway, which is now the island's airport, was a grass field until rebuilt later in the war for Fleet Air Arm torpedo training. Few of the crashed aircraft originated locally – the mountainous island, often wreathed in cloud, was at the cross-roads of many navigational training routes from airfields on the mainland and was an ever present hazard to aircraft in transit between England and Northern Ireland.

The North Barrule has much evidence on its slopes, the most melancholy being the crater made by a B-17G Fortress on 23rd April 1945. The death toll of 31 was the second highest suffered in any high ground crash in Britain up to the present day.

For the record, the worst was the Bristol Wayfarer accident on Winter Hill in Lancashire on 27th February 1958 when 35 of the 42 on board lost their lives. The aircraft, G-AICS, was flying from Ronaldsway to Ringway.

Another Fortress hit a hill near Spanish Head on 14th April 1945 but the site was close to habitation and was cleared without difficulty. Other American losses were two B-24 Liberators on ferry flights from support bases in Northern Ireland and a B-26C Marauder in which six of the eight on board were killed.

One of the Liberators flew into the summit of Snaefell, as did a Wellington II in October 1941. With a railway to the top and a road nearby, the wreckage was soon removed but no doubt, some pieces may have been overlooked.

It was the humble Anson which suffered most, no less than 15 coming to grief on the island hills up to 1961. Their relatively low cruising speed saved many airmen and on one occasion in November 1944 an Anson night-flying from Millom ended up on Snaefell with no injury to her crew. A badly injured wireless operator who had crawled from an Anson wreck on Slieau Ruy in January 1946 was found by a dog which alerted its master.

Regrettably, the island continued to take a toll of aircraft after the war, one of the largest being a Halifax 8 of Lancashire Aircraft Corporation in 1948. It was taking part in an airlift of milk from Ulster to the mainland to relieve a shortage and failed to clear the summit of Cronk Ny Arree Laa by only a few feet. A patch of bare earth strewn with small pieces marks the spot and, half a mile away, some spars from Rapide G-AIUI are built into a dry stone wall.

On the steep seaward slopes of the same hill, a Cherokee 181 crashed in 1982 in approximately the same position as the wartime Marauder. The previously unidentified crash on Beinn-Y-Phott Mountain which was attended by Jurby's ambulance crew on 8th August 1944, is now known to be yet another Anson.

Above: **Anson T.20 VM418** shortly after impact with Clagh Ouyr. All four on board were killed, including the Station Commander at Jurby. G Kniveton via Dave Earl.

AVRO ANSON

30.07.40	L7963	SAN	Dalby Mt. Navex from St Athan. All crew survived.	95/24-78-	X
17.01.42	N5030	27 OTU	Snaefell. Navex from Lichfield.		X
13.02.42	N5346	5 AOS	North Barrule. Navex from Jurby.		X
17.07.42	R9640/81	SPTU	North Barrule. Navex from Cark.		X
19.08.42	N4902	2 OAFU	Snaefell. Navex from Millom.		X
16.12.42	R3432	2 OAFU	Mullagh Ouyr. Navex from Millom.	95/40-86-	X
03.05.43	R9604/62	4 AOS	South Barrule. Navex from West Freugh.		X
13.06.44	EG233	1 OAFU	North Barrule. Navex from Wigtown.		X
01.08.44	EG437	3 SGR	Slieau Ouyr. Navex from Squires Gate.	95/43-88-	X
08.08.44	EG325	3 SGR	Beinn-Y-Phott.		X
13.11.44	AX177/17	10 AFU	Cronk Ny Arree Laa. Navex from Wigtown.		X
15.11.44	EG416	2 OAFU	Snaefell . Navex from Millom. All crew survived.		X
03.01.46	MG445	5 ANS	Slieau Ruy. Navex from Jurby.	95/44-87-	X
05.09.53	VM418/A	1 ITS	Clagh Ouyr. Millom/Jurby.	95/41-89-	X
20.02.61	VL312	TTCCF	North Barrule. Wyton/Aldergrove.		X

BAe HAWK

24.06.83	XX166	4 FTS	Clagh Ouyr. Low-level navex Valley/Lossiemouth		X

BOEING B-17G FORTRESS

23.04.45	43-38856		North Barrule. 31 killed. Ridgewell/Nutts Corner.	95/442908	S
		381st BG			

Above: **Burnt out wreck of B-17G 43-38856 on North Barrule, two days after the crash. It was flying out of Ridgewell to Nutts Corner in Northern Ireland. All 31 on board perished.** D R Osborne via Dave Earl.

CONSOLIDATED B-24 LIBERATOR

09.06.44	42-51202		Snaefell. Ferrying Langford Lodge?/Mainland.		S
	311th FYS				
06.07.44	42-50762	–	North Barrule. From or to Langford Lodge.	95/433904	X

DE HAVILLAND DRAGON RAPIDE

15.08.47	G-AHKR	–	Greeba Mt. Speke/Ronaldsway.	95/321813	X
10.06.48	G-AIUI	–	Cronk Ny Arree Laa. Elmdon/Ronaldsway.	95/225748	X

HANDLEY PAGE HALIFAX

28.09.48	G-AJNZ	LAC	Cronk Ny Arree Laa. Nutts Corner/Speke.	95/223746	X

HANDLEY PAGE HAMPDEN

01.01.40	P1260	7 Sqn	Snaefell. Navex from Upper Heyford.		X

HAWKER HURRICANE

08.10.41	Z3253	133 Sqn	North Barrule. Sealand/Eglinton.	95/38-82-	X
06.02.45	LF693	776 Sqn?	Slieu Ree. Ronaldsway based?	95/?-	

LOCKHEED HUDSON

09.09.41	N7337	1 OTU	North Barrule. Navex from Silloth.		X
21.09.42	AM608/B77	1 OTU	Slieu Freoaghane. Navex from Silloth.	95/34-88-	X

MARTIN B-26 MARAUDER

| 04.07.44 | 41-35791 | | Cronk Ny Arree Laa. Northern Ireland/ | |
| | 449th BS/322nd BG | | Andrews Field? | X |

PIPER CHEROKEE

| 30.10.82 | G-DJMS | – | Cronk Ny Arree Laa. Newtonards/Ronaldsway | X |

SUPERMARINE SPITFIRE

| 14.12.43 | EN856 | 303 Sqn | Snaefell area. Training flight from Ballyhalbert. | X |

VICKERS WELLINGTON

| 08.10.41 | Z8424 | 8 FPP | Snaefell. Ferrying. Hawarden/Aldergrove. | X |
| 23.12.44 | MF174 | EANS | South Barrule. Navex from Shawbury. | X |

Below: **The remains of RB-29 44-61999** *Over Exposure* **were widespread on Higher Shelf Stones in the Peak District, as seen in this July 1984 view. They have since been 'tidied', see page 62.** Alan Curry

Chapter Ten

PEAK DISTRICT

The name of this area conjures up an image of jagged mountains but is very misleading as it consists entirely of moorland up to about 2,000ft with some rocky outcrops and cliffs– the so-called edges. The heights can be treacherous in winter and even in summer when mist descends. Much of the Peak is private land and only the 2½ inch OS shows which this is. I have, therefore, deleted certain map references to avoid conflict with land owners. Access to the moors is restricted on up to 12 days during the grouse shooting season,12th August to 10th December.

Ron Collier of Glossop has published several books about the Peak wrecks which tell survivors' stories and include much information about each incident. Thanks to Ron, the mystery Liberator on Mill Hill has now been identified as an aircraft being ferried from the Base Air Depot at Burtonwood, the two crew escaping with minor injuries. The pilot, with only about 4½ hours in instrument flying in the previous six months, was trying to stay below cloud.

The other Liberator in the Peaks is now known to be a US Navy PB4Y-1 which became completely lost with radio failure whilst returning from an anti-submarine patrol out of Dunkeswell in Devon. The crew baled out over Lincolnshire and luckily the aircraft ran out of fuel over the moors before it reached Manchester.

The V-1 flying-bomb on Margery Hill consists of a large crater and a few scraps of metal, all that remains of a weapon air launched from a Heinkel He111 off the East Coast. It was one of a number aimed at Manchester on Christmas Eve 1944 but few reached their target. There is rumoured to be a German bomber somewhere in the same area which was shot down during a raid on Sheffield. Many years ago, a friend of mine found a 13mm cartridge case of German origin on these moors.

A concentration af interesting wrecks can be found in the vicinity of Higher Shelf Stones within easy reach of the Snake Pass road. The photo-reconnaissance version of the Superfortress had once served with the 509th Composite Group, the unit responsible for the atomic bomb attacks on Japan. A Canadian Lancaster had crashed about three years before, but there is little sign of the aircraft today. Strewn down Ashton Clough are the substantial remains of a C-47 Skytrain which was carrying a Jeep, as springs and transmission parts have been found here.

An element of mystery surrounds the Defiant I on Bleaklow as bullet holes were found in the wreckage. It may hare been shot down but it seems more likely that it simply flew into high ground, perhaps after a brief skirmish with a confused Spitfire which had strayed into its path. Much of the remains were salvaged initially by the RAF Museum but are now in the hands of the Boulton Paul Association and under restoration in Wolverhampton.

Shining Tor is close to the Cat and Fiddle Inn on the Macclesfield to Buxton road on which the crew of a Defiant were found wandering one morning They were somewhat dazed, having flown into the hill in the dark at an angle flat enough for the fighter to remain in one piece. The same squadron, No.96 at Cranage near Middlewich, had already lost another Defiant in the Peaks when the engine failed at night and the crew had to take to their parachutes.

On the southern fringe of the Peak is the striking ridge known as The Roaches. There were several crashes here but it is reasonably accessible and only fragments are left. Investigators should not be surprised if they encounter a wallaby on this hill; a pair escaped many years ago and started a thriving colony which is now in decline!

A number of aircraft returning from bombing operations crashed in the Peaks. The most northerly was the Pathfinder Mosquito B.XVI on its way back from Hamburg to its base near Cambridge. Lost and circling on one engine, trying to find their position, the crew were unlucky enough to fly into a cliff face. The crew of a Wellington III belonging to a Canadian squadron were more fortunate when the aircraft bounced to a halt on a flat portion of Blackden Edge. They had been on a raid over Lorient in Occupied France and were heading for base in North Yorkshire. A Wellington IC of No.150 Squadron crashed on Upper Tor whilst coming back from a Belgian target. It was not far from the spot where a HP Heyford came down before the war.

Below: **Cheetah engine from Anson XI NL185 on The Cloughs.** Dave Earl

AIRSPEED CONSUL

12.04.51	TF-RPM		Outer Edge. Delivery flight Croydon/Prestwick/Iceland.	110/175996 S

AIRSPEED OXFORD

18.10.43	LX518	17 PAFU	Outer Edge. Navex from Wheaton Aston.	110/180968 S
12.03.44	LX745	17 PAFU	Shining Tor. Cross-country from Calveley.	110/998747 S
14.04.45	L4601	17 SFTS	Shutlingsloe.	110/97-69- S
28.12.45	HN594	21 PAFU	Brown Knoll. Navex from Seighford.	TM/082852 S

AVRO ANSON

31.03.41	N9912	25 OTU	Whitwell Moor. Navex from Finningley.	110/249976 S
11.12.44	N9853	10 SFTS	Edale Moor. Newton/Millom.	110/102883 S
23.11.45	NL185	Bmbr	The Cloughs. Halton/Feltwell.	
		Cmd Comms Flt		110/089867 S

AVRO LANCASTER

03.01.45	NF908	467 Sqn	The Roaches. Training flight from Waddington.	119/002636 S
18.05.45	KB993/	408 Sqn	Jame's Thorn.Local flying from Linton-on-Ouse.	110/080946 S
	EQ-U			
21.12.48	PA411/	230 OCU	Tintwhistle Knarr. Training flight from Lindholme.	110/035992 S
	A3-U			

BLACKBURN BOTHA

10.12.41	W5103	7 FPP	Bleaklow. Delivery flight Sherburn-in-Elmet/Hawarden.	110/110972 M

BOEING B-17G FORTRESS

02.01.45	43-38944		Birchenough Hill. Ferrying Burtonwood/	118/996676
		389th BG	Nuthampstead	
06.04.45	43-37667	709th	Meltham Moor.Training flight from Rattlesden.	
		BS/447th BG		110/069096 M

BOEING SUPERFORTRESS

03.11.48	44-61999	16th PR	Higher Shelf Stones. Named *Over Exposed*.	
		Sqn	Scampton/Burtonwood (RB-29J?)	110/091947 L

BOULTON PAUL DEFIANT

13.04.41	N1766	96 Sqn	Rowlee Pasture. Engine failure at night. Crew baled out.	
			Cranage .	110/151905 S
29.08.41	N3378	255 Sqn	Bleaklow. Believed shot at in error by a Spitfire and	
			damaged. Hibaldstow/Turnhouse .	110/106957 M
16.10.41	T3921	96 Sqn	Shining Tor. Local flying from Cranage. Crew survived.	118/998738 S

BRISTOL BLENHEIM

30.01.39	L1476	64 Sqn	Sykes Moor. Familiarisation flight from Church Fenton.	110/080970 L

CONSOLIDATED B-24 LIBERATOR

09.10.44	42-94841	857th	Twizle Head Moss.Training flight from Harrington.	110/106034 S
		BS/492nd BG		
11.10.44	42-52003	27th	Mill Hill. Ferrying Burtonwood/Hardwick	TM/058906 L
		ATG		

Above: **Part of the crash site of RB-29** *Over Exposed* **on Higher Shelf Stones, July 1984.** Alan Curry.

Below: **The site as it presently appears, including memorial stone.** N B Care

Above: **Dragon Rapide G-ALBC on Kinder Scout soon after its demise.** via T Allonby

Below: **Part of the scattered wreckage of the C-47A Skytrain on James's Thorn.** Alan Curry

CONSOLIDATED PB4Y-1 LIBERATOR

| 22.12.43 | 63934 | VB-110 | Irontongue Hill. Radio failure, lost returning after anti-sub patrol from Dunkeswell, diverting to Beaulieu. Crew baled out. | 110/017009 M |

DE HAVILLAND CANADA CHIPMUNK

| 03.07.51 | WB579/16 | 22 RFS | Arnfield Moor. Local flight from Barton. | 110/025946 S |

DE HAVILLAND CANADA L-20A BEAVER

| 05.12.56 | 52-6145 | 81st FBW | Bramah Edge. Sculthorpe/Burtonwood. | 110/050975 S |

DE HAVILLAND DRAGON RAPIDE

| 30.12.63 | G-ALBC | – | Kinder. Caught in downdraught. Middleton St George/Manchester. | 110/102883 S |

DE HAVILLAND MOSQUITO

| 22.10.44 | PF396/ 8K-K | 571 Sqn | Dean Rocks. Lost returning on one engine to Oakington from raid on Hamburg. | 110/026032 S |

DE HAVILLAND TIGER MOTH

| 12.04.45 | T6464 | 24 EFTS | Blindstones Moss. Cross-country from Sealand. | 110/035016 S |

DE HAVILLAND VAMPIRE

| 25.07.51 | WA400 | 102 FRS | Strines Moor. Forced-landing, short of fuel. North Luffenham. | 110/22-89- S |
| 08.08.57 | XE866 | 4 FTS | Moscar Moor. Descending through cloud. | 110/220857 S |

DOUGLAS DAKOTA

| 19.08.49 | G-AHCY | BEA | Wimberry Stones. On instrument approach. Nutts Corner/Ringway. | 110/014025 S |

DOUGLAS C-47A SKYTRAIN

| 24.07.45 | 42-108982/J 314 TCG | | James's Thorn. Amiens/Prestwick. | 110/082946 L |

FAIREY BARRACUDA

| 29.07 .45 | MD963 | NAS Dunino | Red Brook Clough. Pilot was from the Donibristle Ferry Pool. | 110/024103 S |

FAIREY SWORDFISH

| 25.01.40 | P4223 | 819 Sqn | Heydon Head. Missing for a month. Silloth/Ford. | 110/084048 S |

FIESELER FZG.76 (V-1)

| 24.12.44 | – | – | Margery Hill. Air launched towards Manchester by He 111 off East Coast. | 110/185966 S |

GLOSTER METEOR

| 12.04.51 | WA791 and VZ518 | 66 Sqn | Sliddens Moss. Linton-on-Ouse. | 110/069029 L |

Above: **Tail section from one of the two Meteors which collided over Sliddens Moss.** Dave Earl

Below: **Wreckage of 5 PAFU Harvard IIB FT442 shortly after impacting Shining Tor** .

HANDLEY PAGE HALIFAX
05.10.43   HR727/V   51 Sqn   Ashop Moor. Lost, short of fuel returning to Snaith from
ops to Frankfurt.   110/132878 S

HANDLEY PAGE HAMPDEN
30.09.40   L4189   106 Sqn   Black Edge. Night navex from Finningley.   110/098058
23.05.40   L4055/   83 Sqn   Dearden Moss. Returning Scampton from ops.   100/098058 S
            OL-B
21.01.42   AE381   50 Sqn   Cluther Rocks. Lost on cross-country from
Skellingthorpe.   110/08-97- S

HANDLEY PAGE HEYFORD
22.07.37   K6875   166 Sqn   Broadlee Bank Tor. Night exercise from Leconfield.   110/111860 S

HAWKER HURRICANE
22.02.45   PZ765 and   Tintwhistle Knarr. Formation practice from Calveley.
            PZ851 and PZ854l   All from 11 PAFU   110/040993 S

LOCKHEED P-38J LIGHTNING
10.05.44   42-67207496th FTG   Tintwhistle Knarr. Training flight from Goxhill.   110/040993 S

MILES HAWK TRAINER
28.07.57   G-AJSF   –   Kinder Low End. Squires Gate/Barton.   110/074863 S

MILES MASTER
15.01.43   W8840   7 FPP   Near Leek. Ferrying   119/?   X

NORTH AMERICAN HARVARD
30.11.44   FT442   5 PAFU   Shining Tor. Cross-country from Tern Hill.   118/998744 S
14.01.52   FT415   22 FTS   Wool Packs. Syerston/Kemble.   110/090868 S

NORTH AMERICAN MUSTANG
29.05.45   44-72181   4th FG   Castleshaw Valley. Debden/Speke   110/998107 S

NORTH AMERICAN (CANADAIR) F-86 SABRE
25.07.54   XD707 and   Ashop Moor. On an exercise from Linton-on-Ouse.   110/072902 M
            XD730   66 Sqn
14.12.54   19349   421 Sqn/   Holme Moss. North Luffenham/Ringway.   110/090050 S
                    RCAF

REPUBLIC P-47C THUNDERBOLT
25.04.43   41-6227/   78th FG   Horshill Tor. Loss of control in cloud flying Speke/
            UN-F   Horsham St Faith.   110/093845 S

SHORT STIRLING
21.07.44   LJ628   1654 HCU   Upper Commons. Navex from Wigsley.   110/206959 M

SUPERMARINE SEAFIRE
16.07.49   SP314/3251831 Sqn   Wildboarclough. Formation flight from Stretton.   118/999675 S

SUPERMARINE SPITFIRE

17.11.40	P7593	4 FPP	The Roaches. Ferrying Kirkbride/West Malling?	119/00-63- X

VICKERS WELLINGTON

31.07.41	W5719/ JN-S	150 Sqn	Upper Tor. Became lost returning to Snaith after abandoning raid on Cologne owing to bad weather.	110/111876 S
26.01.43	X3348	427 Sqn	Blackden Edge. Returning to Croft from ops to Lorient. All crew survived.	110/128876 S
30.01.43	R1011	28 OTU	Birchen Bank Moss. Navex from Wymeswold.	110/106987 S
22.10.52	MF627	6 ANS	Rod Moor. Navex from Lichfield.	110/26-88- S

WESTLAND LYSANDER

19.08.41	V4903	6 AACU	Slate Pit Moss. Flew reciprocal on night exercise from Sealand.	110/041033-S

Above: **Wing from 66 Squadron Sabre F.4 XD730 on Ashop Moor.** John Grech
Below: **J-47 turbojet from either XD707 or XD730 on Ashop Moor.** Alan Curry

Chapter Eleven

NORTH WALES

Although dominated by Snowdonia, North Wales possesses a number of outlying ranges of considerable magnitude. These include the Berwyns, the so-called Harlech Dome, the Arans and Cadair Idris and its extensive foothills. There are also the many areas of high moorland, the most dangerous to aircraft being Minera Mountain which rises steeply from the edges of the Cheshire and Shropshire Plains.

The few wartime airfields were confined to Anglesey and the coastal strip. Valley was and still is the most important, doubling as a fighter station and Trans-Atlantic Terminal for the USAAF. Mona and Bodorgan were the other Anglesey aerodromes, the former teaching air gunnery and later, navigation, the latter supplying towed targets for local ranges. Towyn was another target towing aerodrome and Llanbedr, built as a fighter base, became an Armament Practice Camp for fighter squadrons.

It was from Llandwrog and Penrhos, however, that most of Snowdonia's victims originated. Penrhos, near Pwllheli, had been a pre-war bombing school and Llandwrog, close to Caernarfon, became its satellite, although planned as a forward fighter station. The roles were later reversed with Llandwrog becoming the parent aerodrome, both concentrating on the training of navigators for Bomber Command.

Despite being far away from significant interference by the Luftwaffe, it was not a happy choice of locations from which to allow trainee navigators to learn by their mistakes. Many of the exercises were carried out at night, often in poor weather, with tragic results. Soon, as a warning to the pupils, there was a map in the control tower at Llandwrog liberally sprinkled with red crosses, each marking an Anson crash in the mountains. So numerous were the accidents, not only to locally-based aircraft but to strangers as well, that a mountain rescue unit had to be formed and became the model for many similar units within the RAF.

The Fortress in the Berwyns was probably the first aircraft of its type lost in the UK by the 8th Air Force and the one near Barmouth amongst the last. An aircraft which almost came to grief in the Berwyns was a USAAF Douglas C-47 which bent *both* wingtips on a mountain top but managed to limp to RAF Montford Bridge in Shropshire for a wheels-up landing.

A particularly tragic incident was the loss of a formation of three Spitfires on a training flight from Llanbedr. In the same area, Wellington IC R1068 of No.21 OTU crashed on 17th August 1941 and its crew are commemorated on a plaque at Pennal Church. There seems to be no trace of the accident on nearby Rhos Fach Mountain, however.

Other memorials in North Wales can be found in the Llanberis Pass in remembrance of the B-26G Marauder crew on Y Garn, on the summit of Arenig Fawr where a B-17G Fortress crashed on a night practice flight, and on Moelfre above Penmaenmawr where a B-24J Liberator hit the mountain.

On the Carnedd Range there was a large concentration of crashes and, such is the spread of wreckage, it is often difficult to establish the identity of the aircraft from which they came. Llyn Dulyn – the Black Lake – and its immediate surroundings, became notorious as a graveyard of aeroplanes. The wing centre section from a USAAF C-47 was a grim landmark for decades until it was dislodged from the cliff to join the rest of the aircraft in the lake. Since the second edition of this guide appeared, many of the aircraft engines have been removed from Snowdonia by helicopter in a misguided tidying-up operation. The only consolation is that they have gone to museums, but they would have been better left as memorials.

For an absorbing account of the stories behind the crashes in Snowdonia, the reader is recommended to obtain a copy of Edward Doylerush's book *No Landing Place*, published by sister company Midland Counties Publications (MCP). Eddie has contacted many of the survivors, analysed the possible causes, and described how the rescue services developed. *Fallen Eagles*, a sequel covering crash sites in other parts of North and mid-Wales is also published by MCP.

It should be emphasised that the whole expanse of Snowdonia and its outliers is potentially dangerous to the unwary walker. In winter, conditions can be suicidal and bad weather can be encountered at any time of the year, often with little pre-warning.

AIRSPEED OXFORD

03.08.41	N4568	11 SFTS	Sychant Pass. Solo flight from Shawbury.	115/757769 S
03.08.42	R6179	USAAF	Vron Hen. Speke/ Langford Lodge.	116/17-60 S
15.11.42	BM824	11 PAFU	Moel Sych. Navex from Shawbury.	125/06-32- X
20.02.44	X7064	11 PAFU	Moel-y-Gamelin. Night cross-country from Calveley.	S
13.01.45	LB537	418 Sqn	Cornel. 50 miles off course. Found by shepherd 05.02.45. Blackbushe/Squires Gate.	115/703670 S

ARMSTRONG WHITWORTH WHITLEY

26.09.42	BD232	24 OTU	Foel Fras. Night cross-country from Honeybourne.	115/703671 M

AUSTER AOP.6

21.10.56	VF554/G	663 Sqn	Bera Mawr. Operating on exercise from landing strip at Aber.	115/679689 M

AVRO ANSON

07.09.41	N9617	10 OTU	Moel Sych. Navex from Abingdon.	125/06-32- X
07.01.42	N9562	9 AOS	Cwm Silyn. Navex from Llandwrog.	115/51-50 S
20.04.42	N4980	9 AOS	Foel Fras. Navex from Llandwrog. Three survived.	115/69-67- X
21.08.42	N4966	CNS	One mile west of Garth. Navex from Cranage.	117/? X
20.11.42	N4981	9 OAFU	Moel Eilio. Navex from Penrhos.	115/55-58- S
28.11.42	DJ635	9 OAFU	Foel Gron. Night navex from Llandwrog.	115/56-56- X
13.01.43	EG110	9 OAFU	Foel Grach. Navex from Llandwrog. Two survived.	115/69-66- X
23.08.43	N5371/AK	9 OAFU	Foel Fras. Navex from Llandwrog. All crew survived.	115/699678 X
05.10.43	LT184	7 AOS	Mynydd Perfedd. Navex from Bishops Court.	115/626622 S
08.11.43	N9855	3 OAFU	Pen yr Ole Wen. Night navex from Halfpenny Green.	115/660622 S
20.11.43	MG111/N	4 AGS	Cwm Silyn. Based Morpeth.	115/520507 S
30.11.43	EF909/J3	5 AOS	Foel Grach. Night navex from Jurby. All crew survived.	115/691667 X
20.02.44	LT433/MI	SPTU	Llyn Cowlyd. Navex from Cark. Four crew survived.	115/727636 S
25.04.44	AX583	2 OAFU	Drum. Navex from Millom.	115/715698 S
08.06.44	LT116	9 OAFU	Mynedd Perfedd. Navex from Llandwrog.	115/625623 S
13.06.44	EG472/CW	9 OAFU	Moel Hebog. Night navex from Llandwrog. One survived.	115/568470 M

12.07.44	MG804	8 OAFU	Foel Fras. Night navex from Mona. Four crew survived.	115/699675 X
11.08.52	VM407	23 MU	Snowdon. Aldergrove/Llandow.	115/607548 S
20.05.59	VV955	CCCS	Tal-y-Fan. Diverting to Valley, Bovingdon/Ballykelly.	115/722722 M

AVRO LANCASTER

| 16.11.42 | W4326 | 101 Sqn | Dolwen Hill. Navex from Holme-on-Spalding Moor | 125/955095 M |
| 06.02.45 | NE132 | 1653 HCU | Rhinog. Broke up in CuNim cloud on navex from North Luffenham. | 124/632285 M |

AVRO LINCOLN

| 15.03.50 | RF511 | 230 OCU | Cwm Llafar. Navex from Scampton, diverting to Valley. | 115/679638 M |

BLACKBURN BOTHA

| 23.08.42 | L6318 | 3 SGR | Tal-y-Fan. Navex from Squires Gate. | 115/72-72 S |
| 28.08.43 | L6202/6-20 | 11 RS | Llwydmor. Training flight from Hooton Park. | 115/683694 M |

BLACKBURN SKUA

| 19.02.41 | L3054 | 801 Sqn | Elidir Fach. West Freugh/St Merryn. | 115/611615 S |

BOEING B-17 FORTRESS

11.08.42	41-9098	340th BS/ 97th BG	Cadair Bronwen. Training flight from Grafton Underwood.	125/079342 S
04.08.43	42-3124	303rd BG	Arenig Fawr. Night training flight from Molesworth.	125/826369 S
08.06.45	44-8639	511th BS/ 351st BG	Craig Cwm Llydd. Polebrook/Valley.	124/645122 S

BRISTOL BEAUFIGHTER

08.09.41	X7640	2 FPP	Moel Siabod. Ferrying Weston/Sealand.	115/714552 S
03.11.43	NE203	2 FPP	Worlds End. Ferrying Weston/Sealand.	117/243483 S
10.02.45	RD210	1 FU	Aran Fawddwy. Fuel consumption test from Pershore.	125/863225 M

BRISTOL BLENHEIM

23.03.40	L4873	90 Sqn	Foel Wen. Cross-country from Upwood.	125/102324 M
09.04.40	L9039/	13 OTU	Craig Yr Ysfa. Cross-country from Bicester.	115/694638 M
31.03.43	V6099	13 OTU	Marchlyn Mawr. On cross-country from Bicester. Not found for twelve days.	115/609621 S

CESSNA 310

| 29.09.68 | G-ARMK | – | Carnedd Dafydd. Leavesden/Squires Gate. | 115/667628 S |

CESSNA 337

| 08.06.79 | G-ATNY | – | Moel Siabod. Coventry/Ronaldsway. | 115/706545 S |

CONSOLIDATED B-24H LIBERATOR

| 18.03.45 | 42-95036 | 801st BG | Disgynfa. Night navex from Harrington.. | 125/053290 S |

CONSOLIDATED B-24J LIBERATOR

| 07.01.44 | 42-99991 | – | Moelfre. Named *Batchelor's Baby*. Transit flight Valley/Watton. Six survived. | 115/716746 S |

DE HAVILLAND MOSQUITO

09.02.44	LR412	540 Sqn	Aran Fawddwy. Cross-country from Benson.	125/859213 M
25.09.44	HX862	60 OTU	Drum. Night navex from High Ercall.	115/716692 M
01.11.44	W4088	51 OTU	Mynydd Mawr. Night navex from Cranfield.	115/543552 M
31.07.48	TV982	502 Sqn	Snowdon. In thunderstorm. Horsham St Faith/ Aldergrove.	115/609528 M

Above: **Mosquito PR.IX LR412 served with 541 Squadron before joining 540 Squadron – both based at Benson. It crashed on Aran Fawddwy on 9th February 1944.**

Below: **One of its Merlin engines is now preserved as part of a memorial cairn outside a farm in the valley.** via Eddie Doylerush

Above: **Tail section of Boston III on Carnedd Dafydd, below the Black Ladders Cliffs. Much of the remains have since been salvaged to help a restoration project.**

DE HAVILLAND QUEEN BEE
24.02.42	V4793	1 AACU	Snowdon. Got out of radio control on pilotless flight from Bodorgan.	115/599553	S

DE HAVILLAND VAMPIRE
07.11.51	WA305	202 AFS	Near Ruabon. Valley.	117/?	X
19.04.56	VV601	7 FTS	Llyn Cowlyd. Local flying from Valley.	115/72-66-	X
12.10.56	VZ874/19	7 FTS	Mynydd Mawr. Night flying from Valley.	115/539547	X
18.04.66	5C-YA	Austrian AF	Mynydd Tarw. Test flight from Hawarden.	125/11-32-	S

DOUGLAS BOSTON
17.10.42	Z2186	418 Sqn	Carnedd Dafydd. Cross-country from Bradwell Bay. Pilot survived.	115/667629	S

DOUGLAS C-47 SKYTRAIN
23.08.42	41-7803	64 TCG	Moel Morfydd. Prestwick/Atcham with personnel for the 14th FG.	117/16-46-	S
12.11.44	43-48473	27 ATG	Craig-y-Dulyn. Diverting to Valley due to fog. Le Bourget/Burtonwood.	115/698667	S

ENGLISH ELECTRIC CANBERRA
09.12.57	WK129	RRE	Carnedd Llewelyn. Trials from Pershore.	115/685647	M

FAIREY BATTLE
16.02.41   L5755   HQSFP   Godor, Berwyn Mts.   125/?   X

FAIREY FULMAR
05.02.41   N4076   Minera Mountain.Ferrying from Worthy Down   117/262511 S

GRUMMAN AVENGER
03.02.44   FN821/4K 848 Sqn   Trum-y-Fawnog. Gosport/Machrihanish.   125/013257 S

HANDLEY PAGE HALIFAX
03.09.44   JD417   1656 HCU   Yr Eifl. Navex from Lindholme.   123/365448 S

HAWKER HART
12.02.37   K4931   5 FTS   Minera Mt. Grantham/Sealand.   117/?   X

HAWKER HENLEY
17.10.40   L3351   1 AACU   Yr Eifl. Towyn.   123/36-44- S
20.11.42   L3334   1605 Flt   Cwm Silyn. Target-towing from Towyn.   115/516502 S

HAWKER HURRICANE
28.01.42   V7001   TFPP   Minera Mt. Ferrying Hanworth/Hawarden.   117/?   S
09.08.42   P3385   MSFU   Allt Fawr. Speke/Valley.   115/681468 X

HEINKEL He 111H-5
14.04.41   F4801/   3/KG28   Llwydmor. Raid on Barrow-in-Furness from Nantes.
          IT+EL   115/684698 S

JODEL DR.250
22.08.69   G-AVIV   –   Carnedd Dafydd. Off course Birmingham/Dublin.   115/664629 S

LOCKHEED HUDSON
04.02.43   AM832   1 OTU   Llechog. Night navex from Silloth.   115/596537 S

LOCKHEED P-38F LIGHTNING
12.02.44   42-12579   27th   Berwyn Mts. Ferrying from Nuthampstead
                      ATG   to Warton.   125/038295 S

LOCKHEED VENTURA
18.08.43   AE688/   464 Sqn   Carnedd Dafydd. Night cross-country from Sculthorpe.
          SB-Q   115/659629 S

MARTIN B-26G MARAUDER
01.02.45   44-68072   Y Garn. Ferrying St Mawgan/Burtonwood.
               Unassigned   Wreckage scattered down Cwm Cwyion from ridge. 115/628598 S

MILES MASTER
30.10.40   N7442   5 SFTS   Minera Mt. Sealand.   117/266493 S
28.07.43   AZ714   17 PAFU   Rhobell Fawr. Cross-country from Calveley.   124/79-26- S

NORTH AMERICAN HARVARD
19.03.51	FX249	502 Sqn	Hope Mt.	117/280584	S

NORTH AMERICAN P-51D MUSTANG
05.05.45	FX898	61 OTU	Minera Mt. Cross-country from Rednal.	117/239463	S
17.05.45	44-726844		Aran Fawddwy. Dived out of formation probably		
		335th FS/4th FG	due to oxygen starvation. Debden	125/?	S

PIPER TWIN COMANCHE
22.10.72	G-AVFV	–	Crib-y-Ddysgl. Southend/Valley.	115/61-55-	

REPUBLIC P-47 THUNDERBOLT
04.05.44	42-75101	495th FTG	Mynydd Copog. Dived into high ground. Atcham.	125/884143	M
08.07.44	41-6195/552nd FTS/ VM-C	495th FTG	Denbigh Moors. Pilot baled out in spin. Atcham. 'Bar' above 'C' in code.	116/916593	S
16.09.44	41-6246	495th FTG	Aran Fawddwy. Found by a shepherd a week later. Atcham	125/862222	M
18.07.43	42-7897	6th FW	Glyndyfrdwy. Atcham.	125/151409	S

SUPERMARINE SPITFIRE
26.05.41	R6834	57 OTU	Cwm Cwmorthin. Apparently descended through cloud. Hawarden.	115/67-46-	S
03.07.41	K9894	57 OTU	Ruabon Mt. Hawarden.	117/24-46-	X
03.07.41	X4167	57 OTU	Ruabon Mt. Hawarden.	117/24-46-	X
26.09.41	X4843	57 OTU	Yr Aran. Hawarden.	115/605517	S
16.11.41	X4713	57 OTU	Ruabon Mt. Local flight from Hawarden.	117/?	X
05.04.42	X4239	57 OTU	Cwm Barlwyd. Operational training from Hawarden.	115.71-48-	S
22.10.42	BL518		Tarrenhendre. Training flight from Llanbedr.	135/68-04-	S
	BM573	all			
	R7296	41 Sqn			
14.12.42	P7295	61 OTU	Cadair Bronwen. Cross-country from Rednal.	125/076337	S
31.08.45	TE210	631 Sqn	Worlds End. Llanbedr.	117/242489	S

VICKERS WELLINGTON
06.04.42	P9299	1429 Flt	Nr Llanymawddwy. Cross-country from East Wretham.	125/?	X
28.05.42	HX433	1443 Flt	Mynydd Moel. Fuel consumption test from Harwell.	124/73-13-	S
19.07.42	DV800	27 OTU	Black Ladders. On navex from Lichfield.	115/675635	S
13.02.43	HE466	30 OTU	Foel Grach. Night cross-country from Hixon.	115/692664	S
20.11.43	LB185	3 OTU	Moel Y Croesau. On navex from Haverfordwest.	124/747386	S
22.08.44	HZ699	CNS	Foel. Navex from Shawbury.	126/18-19-	X

WESTLAND LYSANDER
15.12.42	T1655	61 OTU	Cadair Bronwen. Caught in downdraught while searching for missing Spitfire. Rednal.	125/078342	S

Chapter Twelve

MID AND SOUTH WALES

The presence of a Spitfire OTU at Llandow to the west of Cardiff led inevitably to high ground collisions as trainee pilots got lost or wandered into cloud. One of them, Mk.I X4913 in the Brecon Beacons, has the unfortunate distinction of being the longest-missing aircraft in Britain's hills. It disappeared on 3rd November 1941 and was discovered by a farmer rounding up his sheep on 10th July of the following year. This assumes that no other wreck lies undiscovered somewhere in the wilder parts of the Scottish Highlands – an unlikely possibility, however.

Virtually the whole of the area is mountainous, the Brecon Beacons being the most formidable of a series of ranges which stretch from Plynlimon south to the Black Mountains. The lesser heights of the Prescelli mountains in the south west are a further hazard to aircraft. The airfields were necessarily confined to the coast and the gentler countryside of Pembrokeshire. To the west, Aberporth was used by target-towing aircraft for the local ranges, there were Coastal Command fields at Carew Cheriton, Dale, Talbenny, St Davids and Brawdy, and training aerodromes at Haverfordwest and Templeton.

Fairwood Common was built as a fighter station for the defence of South Wales. It was supported by Pembrey which later became an Air Gunners School. There was a similar school at Stormy Down, near Porthcawl and towards Cardiff the MUs at St Athan and Llandow. RAF Madley was just across the border in England but close enough to the mountains to ensure that it was often responsible for dealing with crashes.

The Bomber OTUs in the south Midlands tended to send their pupil crews over the same standard cross-country routes night after night in all weathers. One of those flown by No.22 OTU at Wellesbourne Mountford in Warwickshire used a turning point at Fishguard. The track crossed a lot of inhospitable country and at least two of the unit aircraft came down in the mountains. One was Wellington X MF505 on Carreg Goch and a memorial plaque lists the names of the crew. Another memorial can be found near where Wellington IC R1465 crashed in the Beacons during a night navex. In Glyntawe churchyard is a commemorative inscription dedicated to the help rendered by the villagers in searching for the survivors of an Anson crash in 1939.

I did not include the Plynlimon P-38G Lightning in previous editions of this book as it was very accessible, as well as substantially complete, and I feared it would be removed piecemeal. This seems to have happened anyway although happily most of the large sections have found their way to museums. The large code letters 'G2-Q' were visible on the underside of one of the wings and up to about ten years ago, the Lightning was one of the most intact wrecks in Britain.

There are several other American aircraft crash sites in South Wales, including a P-38 which was on a training flight from Andover, a Marauder on a hilltop near St Davids and a US Navy Liberator close to the lonely Glyntawe/Trecastle road. It was on a routine night familiarisation flight from Dunkeswell in Devon and all seven crew were killed.

An attack against targets in north west France on 16th September 1943 resulted in the loss of two B-17Gs and their crews in the Welsh Mountains. *Ascend Charlie* was hit in the No.1 engine by flak but maintained formation until the returning aircraft were forced to scatter when they encountered a weather front in gathering darkness. The damaged aircraft failed to clear the mountains near Abergavenny and all ten crew were killed. *Sondra Kay*, an aircraft of the 388th Bomb Group, was lost in similar circumstances.

For much greater detail and background on most of the Mid and South Wales crashes, the reader is recommended to consult *Warplane Wrecks of South Wales and the Marches* by Peter Durham and Dewi Jones.

AIRSPEED OXFORD

07.01.46	PH242	21 PAFU	Hay Bluff. Engines recovered by 2478 Sqn ATC. Cross-country from Seighford.	161/256358	S
06.12.53	HM784	63 GpCF	Ebbw Vale Mt. Cardiff.	161/18-06-	M

AVRO ANSON

17.01.39	L9149	9 E&R FTS	Bannau Brycheiniog. Navex Hamble/Ansty. Memorial plaque in Glyntawe Churchyard.	160/825214	M
02.03.40	N9879	6 AONS	Black Mts. Navex from Staverton.	161/255354	S
09.07.40	N5019	15 OTU	Near Llanwrthwl. Navex from Harwell.	148/?	X
21.09.42	N9745	6 AOS	Near Llanthony. Navex from Staverton.	161/?	X

AVRO LANCASTER

06.09.43	W4929/ GP-R	1661 HCU	Garn Las. Well scattered. Night navex from Winthorpe.	160/828238	S

AVRO VULCAN

11.02.66	XH536	Con'sby Wg	Fan Bwlch Chwyth. Long trail of wreckage.	161/913215M	

BOEING B-17 FORTRESS

11.04.43	42-29505	–	Prescelli Mts. Named *Gunga Din*. Crew survived.	145/09-31-	X
16.09.43	42-5906	388th BG	Rhiw Gwriadd. Named 'Sondra Kay'. Returning from Bordeaux to Knettishall.	147/01-63	S
16.09.43	42-5903	390th BG	Black Mts. Named 'Ascend Charlie'. Returning from Bordeaux with flak damage. Base Framlingham.	161/243253	

BRISTOL BLENHEIM

22.09.40	L8610	17 OTU	Garn Wen. Navex from Upwood.	161/285046-S	

CONSOLIDATED PB4Y-1 LIBERATOR

24.08.44	38753	VB-110	Moel Feity. Night training flight from Dunkeswell.	160/848230	S

CONSOLIDATED B-24 LIBERATOR

19.09.44	EV881	547 Sqn	Prescelli Mts. On exercise from St Eval. Memorial on site.	145/128317 S

DE HAVILLAND HORNET

30.09.46	PX273	30 MU	Mynydd-y-Glog. On test from St Athan.	160/975094	M

DE HAVILLAND VAMPIRE

09.10.53	VZ106	233 OCU	Bannau Brycheiniog. Pembrey.	160/828204	L

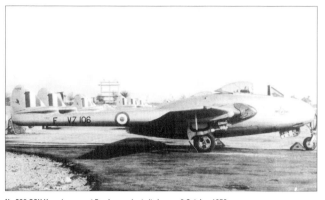

No.233 OCU Vampire seen at Pembrey, prior to its loss on 9 October 1953

FAIREY BATTLE

06.10.38	K7589	226 Sqn	Plynlimon. Cross-country from Harwell.	135/801871 S
26.02.40	K7688	9 BGS	Prescelli Mts. Cross-country from Penrhos to Stormy Down. Crew survived.	145/125326 M

HANDLEY PAGE HALIFAX

22.05.44	LK835	52 Sqn	Waun Afon. Cross-country from Snaith.	161/223103 S
12.12.44	LL541	1664 HCU	Nant-Yr-Haidd. Mid-air break-up. Dishforth.	147/93-66- S

HAWKER HURRICANE

07.01.40	L2074	11 Gp	Mynydd William Meyrick.	170/95-92 S
29.12.40	W9123	1 FPP	1 mile SSW of Maesteg. Shawbury/St Eval.	170/84-90- X
26.09.41	Z3662	79 Sqn	Rhigox. Fairwood Common.	170/94-03- X

JUNKERS Ju 88

25.04.42	3459/ 5K+DW	IV/KG 3	Gwaunceste Hill. Night intruder mission from Brussels-Evere. Shot down by Beaufighter X7933 of 25 Squadron.	148/135549 S

LOCKHEED HUDSON

07.01.40	N7256	233 Sqn	Mynydd Maendy. Base was Leuchars.	170/95-89- X

LOCKHEED P-38G LIGHTNING

11.09.45	42-13345/ G2-Q	7 PG	Plynlimon. Training flight from Chalgrove.	136/797870

LOCKHEED P-38J LIGHTNING

12.04.44	42-67859	402nd FS/370th FG	Olchon Valley. Training flight from Andover.	161/272323 S

Above: **Parts of the USAAF P-38G Lightning on Plynlimon bearing underwing codes 'G2-Q'. It is one of two P-38 crash sites in the region.**

Below: **Small amount of wreckage and memorial to the Canadian crew of 22 OTU Wellington IC R1465 at Waen Rydd.**

MARTIN B-26 MARAUDER

04.06.43	41-34765		Carn Lliddi. Ferrying St Mawgan/Valley.	157/739281-S
		322nd BG		

MILES MARTINET

31.01.44	MS525	7 AGS	3 miles north-east of Port Talbot. Stormy Down.	170/?	X
21.12.45	HN888	595 Sqn	Near Llandindrod Wells. Found by shepherd 02.02.46.		
			Aberporth/Castle Bromwich.		X

NORTH AMERICAN MUSTANG

07.09.45	KH499	118 Sqn	Mynydd-y-Glog. Fairwood Common.	160/969086 S

SUPERMARINE SPITFIRE

06.08.41	X4381	53 OTU	Near Ton-Pentre. Llandow.	170/?	S
12.08.41	R7057	53 OTU	Mynydd Pen-y-Cae. Llandow.	170/?	S
03.11.41	X4913	53 OTU	Pen-y-Fan. Llandow. Wreckage not found until 10.07.42.	161/014215 S
03.01.42	P9491	53 OTU	Mynydd-y-Glyn. Llandow.	170/?	X
08.03.42	L1014	53 OTU	Skirrid Fawr. Spun out of cloud. Llandow.	161/324176 S
23.05.42	X4588	53 OTU	Brecon Beacons. Wreckage found on 02.06.42.		
			Llandow.	161/017184 S

VICKERS WELLINGTON

09.12.40	T2520/	115 Sqn	Cefn Ystrad. Became lost returning from ops		
	KO-A		Bordeaux to Marham.	160/088136 S
06.07.42	R1465/Y	22 OTU	Waen Rydd. Night navex from Wellesborne Mountford.		
			Memorial to all-Canadian crew nearby.	160/062198 M
26.09.42	BJ697	12 OTU	Black Mt. Navex from Chipping Warden.	160/836182 S
20.11.44	MF509	22 OTU	Garreg Goch. Night navex from Stratford.		
			Probably iced up in cloud	161/816171 L

Chapter Thirteen

DARTMOOR, BODMIN AND EXMOOR

Apart from the wrecks on the uplands of South West England, I have included the three sites on Lundy Island for interest, although they are not strictly high ground incidents. There were few local aerodromes around Dartmoor other than Harrowbeer, which was built for the defence of Plymouth and soon found itself supplying mountain rescue facilities. The group of Coastal Command bases in Cornwall were far enough away from the high ground for it not to have much effect on their operations, but not so the US Navy airfield at Dunkeswell in Devon. The Liberator squadrons of Fleet Air Wing 7 and, in the early days, those of the USAAF's anti-submarine units, were forced to overfly Dartmoor to and from their patrols in the Bay of Biscay and the South West Approaches.

Training aircraft were relatively uncommon over this part of the country, a fact which is readily apparent from a study of the listing. One which did crash was the Spitfire XVI on Brent Moor which in the 1950s was visible from the air and recognisable. Unfortunately, for this reason it was subsequently buried. Large portions of a Battle, presumably the one at Two Bridges, were recovered by the RAF in 1964 but it is not known what became of them.

Another mystery is that of the USAAF fighter found near Princetown on 2nd March 1943 where it had crashed the day before. The 8th Air Force was not active on that particular date, so perhaps it was on a training flight. At that stage of the war it was probably a Thunderbolt. On 22nd November 1945, a Vengeance target-tug took off from Exeter for a 30 minute test flight. Neither it nor its pilot were ever seen again. If it did not crash in the Channel, it could have plunged into a Dartmoor bog.

Most of the US Navy PB4Y-1 Liberator on Steeperton Tor was removed by an RAF salvage unit in a wintertime job which took nine days. Another of their subjects was a burnt-out C-54 Skymaster, 42-72249, which had crashed on the moors near Launceston in 1944 whilst inbound to the Trans-Atlantic Terminal at St Mawgan. It was reasonably accessible and was removed with the aid of a sledge and tractor.

Dartmoor was ideally placed to catch stray aircraft returning from raids over North-West France. Two Hampdens from Scampton in Lincolnshire were lost in this way within a fortnight under Hamel Down Tor and Hangingstone Hill. The Lancaster I on Standon Hill, was however, on a training flight, No.207 Squadron having just re-equipped with the type.

Close to Hameldon Tor, on Manaton Hill, is a 6ft standing stone which was erected by two local men. On it are engraved the date and initials of the five British airmen who were killed in the crash of Hampden X3054. The smooth-heathery hilltop site still has tall wooden posts as a wartime deterrent to enemy aircraft landings.

The Beaufighter II in the same area had been on a night patrol from Exeter and evidently descended too soon through cloud. The wreck was salvaged by No.67 MU and one of the former team members tells me that they lost a wheel and a tyre which disappeared into the undergrowth when they deliberately rolled it downhill to save carrying it! Perhaps it lies there still.

Finally, a word of warning. Whilst watching anxiously for spectral hounds you could just wander into one of the infamous morasses. On a more serious note, vast tracts of the Moor are used as an artillery range, some of the wrecks lying within its boundaries. Local enquiry and warning notices will establish when and where it is safe to go. Suspicious objects should given a wide berth, a precaution also to be observed at many crash sites in this book.

ARMSTRONG WHITWORTH WHITLEY
| 01.06.42 | AD698 | 77 Sqn | Lundy. Returning to Chivenor from patrol. | 180/? | S |

AVRO ANSON
| 28.11.39 | N5084 | 148 Sqn | Exmoor. Cross-country from Harwell. | 180.789348 | X |

AVRO LANCASTER
| 24.05.42 | R5617 | 207 Sqn | Standon Hill. Cross-country from Bottesford. | 191/580815- | S |

BOEING B-17G FORTRESS
| 25.12.43 | 42-37869 | 8th AF Weather Flt | Okehampton Moor. St Eval/Cheddington. | 191/?- | X |

BRISTOL BEAUFIGHTER
| 27.09.41 | R2442 | 307 Sqn | Hameldon Tor. On patrol from Exeter. | 191/70-80 | X |
| 03.09.45 | RD558 | 151 RU(A) | Withypool. Warton?/St Athan or Squires Gate. Belgian crew killed. | 181/186344 | X |

BRISTOL BLENHEIM
| 11.06.41 | V5933 | 53 Sqn | Bodmin Moor. St Eval. | 202/? | X |

CONSOLIDATED B-24 LIBERATOR
| 27.12.43 | 42-40474 | 36th BS/ 482nd BG | Hameldon. Training flight from Alconbury. | 191/70-80- | X |

CONSOLIDATED PB4Y-1 LIBERATOR
| 03.12.43 | 32014/G | VB-103 | Steeperton Tor. Mostly cleared. Training flight from Dunkeswell. | 191/62-89- | S |
| 28.12.43 | 63926/E | VB-110 | Okehampton Moor. Anti-shipping strike from Dunkeswell. | 191/568885 | X |

DE HAVILLAND SEA VIXEN
| 31.05.65 | XN648 | 766 Sqn | Rough Tor. Yeovilton. | 191/60-79-- | X |

DE HAVILLAND VAMPIRE
| 25.09.52 | VZ813 | 229 OCU | Dartmoor. Chivenor. | 191/? | S |

DOUGLAS C-47 SKYTRAIN
| 13.10.45 | 42-100640 | 484th ASG | Huntingdon Warren.Erding, Germany/Exeter, diverting to Weston Zoyland. | 202/66-67- | X |

FAIREY BATTLE
| 04.07.39 | K9391 | 150 Sqn | Two Bridges. Cross-country from Benson. | 202/? | X |

FAIREY FULMAR

| 18.01.43 | X8812 | 781 Sqn | Tanners Hill, Dartmoor.St Merryn/Lee-on-Solent | 191/54-93- | X |

GLOSTER GLADIATOR

| 20.11.40 | N5644 | 247 Sqn | Near Okehampton. On patrol from St Eval. | 191/? | X |

GLOSTER METEOR

| 14.10.49 | VW434 | 56 Sqn | Sherden Hill. Thorney Island/Chivenor. | 180/795353 | X |

HANDLEY PAGE HAMPDEN

| 21.03.41 | X3054 | 49 Sqn | Hameldon Tor. Returning to Scampton from ops. | 191/70-80- | X |
| 04.04.41 | AD748 | 83 Sqn | Hangingstone Hill. Returning to Scampton from mine-laying at La Rochelle. | 191/61-86- | X |

HAWKER HUNTER

| 19.03.71 | XG131 | 229 OCU | Near Dulverton. Chivenor. | 181/? | X |

HEINKEL He 111H-5

| 03.03.41 | 3911/ IG+AL | I/KG27 | Lundy. From Tours. | 180/? | M |
| 01.04.41 | 3837/ IG+FL | I/KG27 | Lundy. From Tours. | 180/? | S |

SHORT STIRLING

| 22.08.42 | R9329/V | 149 Sqn | Near Cornwood. Returning to Lakenheath after mining off French Coast. | 202/? | X |

SUPERMARINE SEAFIRE

| 15.03.48 | SX237 | 736 Sqn | Bodmin Moor. St Merryn. | 202/? | X |

SUPERMARINE SPITFIRE

29.11.41	W3968	317 Sqn	Near Princetown. Patrol from Exeter.		X
16.08.42	P9468	53 OTU	3 miles north of Widdicombe. Lost, pilot baled out. Llandow.	202/?	X
06.12.42	EP749	19 Sqn	White Tor. Perranporth.	191/54-79-	X
23.10.47	TE406	203 AFS	Brent Moor. Mainly buried. Chivenor.	202/654640	S

VICKERS WELLINGTON

28.12.41	Z8971	75 Sqn	Dartmoor. Returning to Feltwell from ops Brest	191/?	X
06.10.42	BX281	142 Sqn	Near Princetown. On ops from Waltham		X
01.06.43	MP597	3 OADU	Kitty Tor. Ferrying Boscombe Down?/Gibraltar	191/56-87-	X
01.03.44	LN775	3 OADU	Two Barrows, Dartmoor. Ferrying overseas.		X

Chapter Fourteen

NORTHERN IRELAND

The crash sites in the Province reflect the wide variety of operational and training types based there during the Second World War. Thanks are due to Ernie Cromie and John Quinn for expanding considerably the lists in previous editions. One location not yet traced, however, is where a USAAF B-24 from Cluntoe crashed on 2nd March 1944.

There were 20 active airfields during the last war as well as the flying-boat bases at Castle Archdale and Killadeas on Lough Erne. Coastal Command flew from Aldergrove, Nutts Corner, Ballykelly and Limavady and there were fighter stations at Ballyhalbert and Kirkistown. The USAAF occupied several airfields in a training and support role, Langford Lodge, Cluntoe and Toome being the most important. There was also a Coastal OTU at Long Kesh, a navigation school at Bishops Court and Royal Naval Air Stations at Eglinton and Maydown.

With all this flying going on it is not surprising that there were so many accidents on the extensive high ground to be found over much of the region. One notorious example is the mountain known as Benevenagh which was close to tbe aerodromes along the coastal strip bordering Lough Foyle, dangerously so in the case of Limavady where it rises within the circuit area. It proved fatal to many and Shackleton crews of a later era nick named it 'Ben Twitch'.

The hills around Belfast saw many crashes but it is believed that virtually all wreckage was removed because they are fairly easy to reach. There is certainly evidence of some of them, however, and all known accidents on this high ground have been included for information. The B-17G on Cave Hill was on the final stage of a Trans-Atlantic ferry flight and there were several other losses of British aircraft flying to and from Nutts Corner.

The Coastal OTU at Long Kesh, now the site of The Maze Prison, operated many Beauforts, a few of which flew into hills. The two Mosquitoes from High Ercall in Shropshire were engaged in practice night intruding over Ulster airfields. This was a standard exercise on the curriculum as the Irish Sea crossing could simulate the English Channel. The two Beaufighters lost during 1942 were operational aircraft on night patrols from Ballyhalbert.

The transport aircraft involved in a crash near Maghera in September 1943 is now known to have been a Cessna Bobcat and the commander of the US Navy base at Londonderry was one of the fatal casualties. There were two survivors from the crew of another American aircraft, a Fortress, which came down near Cushendall in 1942.

At least two Marauders from the 3rd Combat Crew Replacement Centre at Toome were wrecked in high ground accidents. This unit gave brief familiarisation in British weather conditions and flying procedures to crews newly arrived from the USA for the 9th Air Force.

As well as the Sunderland on Knocklayd Mountain, there was almost another Sunderland loss in the Province when an aircraft of No.423 Squadron struck a hilltop, severely damaging the hull and leaving pieces which were later removed by No.226 MU. The flying-boat subsequently crash-landed at Jurby aerodrome on the Isle of Man and caught fire. Widespread damage was caused when the depth charges eventually went off.

Navigational exercises were flown constantly over Northern Ireland, often at night, from local airfields and observer schools on the mainland and the Isle of Man. At least six Ansons were lost in the hills in various parts of Ulster during the war years. The solitary Oxford was a squadron 'hack' based at Bal-

lykelly, local people playing an important part in bringing help for the injured crew in appalling weather conditions.

AIRSPEED OXFORD

15.12.44	AS874	59 Sqn	Coolcosreaghan. Ballykelly.	H/79-09-	X

AVRO ANSON

31.01.40	N4943	1 AONS	Near Cushendall. Navex from Prestwick.		S
09.11.42	AX322	1 AOS	4½ miles north west of Moneymore. Navex from Wigtown.		S
18.12.42	DJ572	5 AOS	5 miles north west of Moneymore. Navex from Jurby.		S
23.02.43	EG460	1 OAFU	Brackaghslievegallion. Navex from Wigstown.		S
21.04.44	N5168/Q1	7 OAFU	Near Cushendall. Navex from Bishops Court.		S
06.03.45	LV153	1 OAFU	Mullaghclogha. Navex from Wigtown.		S
07.07.47	NK877	2 ANS	Meenard Mt. Navex from Bishops Court.	H/661980	S

BOEING B-17 FORTRESS

03.10.42	41-24451	91st BG	Slieveanarra Mt. Two survived. Gander/Prestwick.		S
03.06.44	42-97862		Cave Hill. Ferrying Gander/Nutts Corner.	J/32-80-	S

BRISTOL BEAUFIGHTER

26.05.42	X7573	153 Sqn	Near Moneyreagh. Loss of control in cloud. Ballyhalbert.		X
19.07.42	X7822	153 Sqn	Mourne Mts. On night patrol from Ballyhalbert.	J/250214	S

BRISTOL BEAUFORT

20.01.43	L9828	5 OTU	Ballycollin Hill. Operational training from Long Kesh.	J/26-70-	X
29.03.43	AW277	5 OTU	Collin Mt. Operational training from Long Kesh.	J/26-70-	X
17.06.43	JM452	5 OTU	Divis Mt. Operational training from Long Kesh.	J/280753	S
23.07.43	JM451/18	5 OTU	Five miles west of Swatragh, Antrim. Long Kesh.		X

CESSNA UC-78 BOBCAT

04.09.43		USAAF	Near Maghera. C-in-C US Navy Base Londonderry killed. Eglinton/Hendon		X

CONSOLIDATED CATALINA

20.11.44	JX242/P	202 Sqn	Magho Hill, Fermanagh. Anti-sub,Castle Archdale.		X

CONSOLIDATED B-24 LIBERATOR

04.05.42	AL558/B	120 Sqn	Divis Mt. Nutts Corner.	J/270754	S
21.08.42	LV340/X	120 Sqn	Antrim. In bad weather Ballykelly/Nutts Corner. Cleared		S
03.11.42	AL519	120 Sqn	Benevenagh. Night flying practice fr Ballykelly. Cleared		S
24.06.44	FL977/H	59 Sqn	Benevenagh. On approach to Ballykelly.		S
30.01.45	EW628	1332 HCU	Standing Stones Hill. Navex from Nutts Corner.	J/25-74-	X
16.02.45	EV954	1674 HCU	Collindale. Antrim. Navex from Aldergrove. Cleared		X
19.03.45	KG896	1674 HCU	Tornagrough, Antrim. Aldergrove. Cleared.	J/25-73-	X

DE HAVILLAND DOMINIE

15.09.53	NF861	703 Sqn	Glendun Mt. Stretton/Eglinton.		X

DE HAVILLAND HORNET MOTH
31.07.41	W9380	24 Sqn	Sperrin Mts. Reconnoitring AA guns in Londonderry area.	S

DE HAVILLAND MOSQUITO
14.03.44	DZ718	60 OTU	Three miles east of Dromore. Intruder ex, High Ercall.	J/307505	S
13.01.45	NS996	60 OTU	Slieve Commedagh. Intruder ex, from High Ercall.	J/349279	S

FAIREY BATTLE
22.10.40	P6601	226 Sqn	Trostan. Operational patrol from Sydenham.	M

GRUMMAN HELLCAT
06.08.45	–	891 Sqn	Sawell, Sperrin Mts. Night exercise from Eglinton..	X

LOCKHEED HUDSON
16.08.41	AM588	206 Sqn	Four miles NE of Ladyhill, Antrim. Night flying from Aldergrove.		S
04.01.42	AM607	220 Sqn	Agnew's Hill, Antrim..	D/325016	S
12.04.42	V9112	1527 BATF	Crockaneel Mt. From Prestwick		S

MARTIN B-26 MARAUDER
10.04.44		3 CCRC	Mourne Mts. Lost formation during practice flight from Toome.	S
21.06.44		3 CCRC	Slieve Gallison. Believed cleared. Three survived. Toome.	

SHORT SUNDERLAND
05.12.43	W6013	423 Sqn	Knocklayd Mt, Ballycastle. Descended too early through cloud. Castle Archdale. Cleared

STINSON RELIANT
05.01.44	FK914	Eg' Stn Flt	Knockanbone, Sperrin Mts. Eglinton.	X

SUPERMARINE SEAFIRE
02.10.45	SR482	803 Sqn	Slievenanee. Nutts Corner.	D/160218	S

SUPERMARINE SPITFIRE
17.02.43	AB960	501 Sqn	Slieve Greeba. On night cross-country from Ballyhalbert.	X

VICKERS WELLINGTON
16.03.42	X3599	57 Sqn	Thomas Mt. Engines recovered by Ulster Aviation Society 1984. Feltwell/Aldergrove.	J/363293	S
02.01.43	W5713	7 OTU	Binevenagh. In blizzard. Crew survived. Limavady.		S
13.07.43	HF838	7 OTU	Binevenagh. In the circuit for Limavady. Cleared		S
12.09.43	X9820	105 OTU	Slieve Commedagh. On navex from Bramcote.	J/343286	S
17.09.43	W5647	7 OTU	Scawt Hill, Antrim. Navex from Limavady. One killed.	J/33-09-	S
05.11.43	LB247	7 OTU	Binevenagh. In Limavady. Circuit in bad weather. One fatal casualty.		X
24.11.43	Z1313	104 OTU	Divis Mt. On instrument approach to Nutts Corner.	J/28-75-	X
31.12.43	T1520	104 OTU	Rushey Hill, Dunrod. Returning to Nutts Corner from navex.	J/24-72-	X

Chapter Fifteen

IRELAND

Although of course neutral during the Second World War, Eire was overflown frequently, unintentionally or otherwise, by Allied and German aircraft. The mountain ranges along the south and west coasts claimed some of them and so many crashed on Mount Brandon in County Kerry that the British requested a geological survey. It was suspected that mineral deposits were affecting aircraft compasses but no evidence was found to support this theory, nor for the more sinister one that a German agent had placed a decoy radio beacon on the mountain! It seems the real reason was that the high ground was on a long peninsula projecting into the Atlantic.

(For a narrative history of Ireland's 'neutrality' and the aircraft that 'visited' in one form or another during the Second World War, read *Wings over Ireland* by Donal MacCarron, from Midland Publishing.)

Most of the British losses were Coastal Command aircraft from bases in Northern Ireland, the mountains of Donegal being a particular hazard to those straying over neutral territory in bad weather. No.59 Squadron from Ballykelly lost two Liberator GR.Vs here in a single night soon after take off when both failed to clear the high ground. They were loaded with fuel and depth charges and all 16 crew were killed. The Bluestack Mountains claimed a Sunderland III from Pembroke Dock in January 1944 while it was diverting to Lough Erne after an anti-submarine patrol. Local people have painted a simple memorial inscription to the crew on a rock close to the crash site.

Still in Donegal, a Hampden which was returning to base in Lincolnshire after a raid on Germany became hopelessly lost and eventually collided with the Glendowan Mountains. During March 1945, a Sunderland hit a hill near Killybegs just prior to setting course on a U-boat patrol, killing all 12 on board. North west Eire was the scene of another Coastal Command accident after the war when a Halifax VI on a weather sortie came down on Achill Island.

As mentioned above, Brandon Mountain was the downfall of four aircraft. The earliest was a Focke-Wulf Condor in August 1940 which was on a routine long range armed reconnaissance from Bordeaux to Norway. The pilot must have seen the ground at the last moment, pulled the stick back and stalled onto a steep slope. Incredibly only two of the crew were slightly hurt and the wreck was set on fire in customary fashion. Because this was the first German aircraft to crash in Ireland, the military authorities removed much of the wreckage, including three of the engines, for investigation. The site is still well worth a visit however, and a local farmer has adapted pieces as gates and parts of walls, the Luftwaffe camouflage being discernible.

Two Sunderlands crashed on Brandon within a month, the RAF flying boat being on an Atlantic patrol, while the BOAC example was operating the Lisbon-Foynes leg of the company's West Africa service. It was carrying the first PoW mail from Japan and local people painstakingly collected all the scattered letters for onward delivery. Some of the remains from this crash are displayed at the Flying-Boat Museum, Foynes.

Unexploded depth charges could be seen at the RAF Sunderland site until quite recently when the Irish Army finally decided to deal with them! The Wellington nearby had an all-Polish crew, none of whom survived. There was once an intriguing rumour that the remains of a Junkers Ju 52 lay near the Gap of Dunloe in Kerry. It was supposed to have been lost dropping German agents into Eire but the story may have been confused with the French-built Ju 52 (an Amiot AAC-1 Toucan) which crashed in the Wicklow Mountains in 1946. The French Air Force aircraft was flying a party of girl guides to Dublin when it hit high ground, coming to rest virtually intact with no fatalities. It was not salvaged but the ubiquitous tinkers removed it piecemeal and there is said to be nothing left today.

Late in the war, RAF salvage teams were allowed free access to the Republic to recover wreckage and much of what they abandoned was subsequently cleared by the tinkers for its scrap value. Reputedly large remains of a Catalina on Stradbally Mountain were removed quite recently by a local farmer when his sheep suffered from the effects of chewing on lead-covered wiring!

Irish aviation enthusiasts have placed memorials at a number of crash sites in the south of the country, including the Liberator in the Caha Mountains. Another commemorates the crew of a USAAF C-47 which crashed on one of Ireland's highest peaks in a particularly rugged and remote area.

Below: **Wing section, undercarriage leg, turbocharger and engine from B-17G 42-31439 on an Irish mountainside.** John Quinn

BOEING B-17G FORTRESS

9.12.43	42-31439	–	Location withheld for the time being.	L

CESSNA 182

19.11.68	5Y-AIN	–	Slieve Felim, Limerick. Bembridge/Shannon.	X
07.09.85	G-BKGY	–	Blackstairs Mt. Birmingham/Kilkenny.	X

CESSNA 185A

29.06.67	EI-AMT	–	Lugnaquilla, Co Wicklow.	M

CONSOLIDATED CATALINA

21.01.41	AM265	240 Sqn	Glengad Mt. Leitrim. Patrol from Loch Erne.	S
19.12.44	JX208/F	202 Sqn	Stradbally Mt. On anti-sub patrol from Castle Archdale.	S

CONSOLIDATED B-24 LIBERATOR

16.03.42	AL577/N	108 Sqn	Slieve Na Glogh. North Africa/Southern England. Radio unserviceable. Completely lost.	S
27.08.43	BZ802/V	86 Sqn	Caha Mt. Returning to Aldergrove from anti-sub patrol.	M
19.06.44	FL990/A	59 Sqn	Donegal. Anti-sub patrol in bad weather from Ballykelly.	S
19.06.44	FL989/L	59 Sqn	Glengad Head, Donegal. Soon after take-off from Ballykelly on anti-sub patrol.	M

DOUGLAS C-47 SKYTRAIN

17.12.43	43-30719	437th TCG	Cummeenapeasta, Kerry. Ferrying Port Lyautey/St Mawgan. Memorial nearby.	S

FOCKE-WULF Fw 200 CONDOR

20.08.40	F8+KH	III/KG40	Mt Brandon. Operational flight Bordeaux/Norway. Crew all survived.	M

HANDLEY PAGE HALIFAX

16.06.50	RG843/ Y3-0	202 Sqn	Croaghaun, Achill Island. Met sortie from Aldergrove.	M

HANDLEY PAGE HAMPDEN

02.10.41	AD768	106 Sqn	Glendowan Mts. Donegal. Became lost returning to Coningsby from ops to Karlsruhe.	S

HANDLEY PAGE HARROW

14.12.43	K7005	271 Sqn	Inishowen Head..	S

JUNKERS Ju 52 (AAC-1)

12.08.46	No.46/B	Fr AF	Wicklow Mts. All 27 on board survived. Le Bourget/Dublin.	X

JUNKERS Ju 88

03.03.42	1429/ CN+OU	Wek 2	Mt Gabriel, Co Cork. Weather reconnaissance flight from North-west France.	S

LOCKHEED HUDSON

11.01.41	N7298	224 Sqn	Kildare. On patrol from Leuchars.	X
27.09.41	AE577	ATFERO	Near Dundalk. Baldonnel/Prestwick. Cleared	

SHORT SUNDERLAND

28.07.43	G-AGES	BOAC	Mt Brandon. Lisbon/Foynes	S
22.08.43	DD848/N	201 Sqn	Mt Brandon. Anti-sub patrol from Castle Archdale.	M
31.01.44	DW110	228 Sqn	Bluestack Mts. Donegal.	L
14.03.45	ML743/ ZM-A	201 Sqn	Near Killybegs. Outbound on patrol from Castle Archdale.	M

SUPERMARINE SEAFIRE

28.05.51	154	IAC	Carrie Hill, Wicklow Mts. Training flight from Gormanston	X

VICKERS VESPA

18.05.31	V3	IAC	Foxford Mts. Mayo	X

VICKERS WELLINGTON

11.04.41	W5653	221 Sqn	Fort Dunrae, Donegal. Anti-sub patrol from Limavady.	S
20.12.43	HF208	304 Sqn	Mt Brandon. On anti-submarine patrol from Predannack	M

Below: **Aircraft parts are often adapted for domestic purposes, such as this geodetic stream bridge which was once part of Wellington XIV HF208. The object in the foreground is possibly a Leigh Light swivel ring.** John Quinn

MOUNTAIN CODE

1   Plan, with maps.
2   Do not try too much too soon. Move gradually to bigger things.
3   Go with others and keep together always. Until experienced don't take charge of others: then take only ten or less.
4   Equip against the worst. Be well shod: have warm clothing and a waterproof cover, spare clothes and food for all, map, whistle, torch and compass.
5   Give yourself ample time, and more as a reserve. Move steadily. Do not hurry and do not waste time.
6   Do not throw down or dislodge rocks or stones. Know and observe the Country Code.
7   Eye the weather: it can change completely in a few hours. Do not go on recklessly if it turns bad. Do not be afraid to come down.
8   Do not go rock, snow or ice climbing without an experienced leader.
9   If lost do not panic or rush down. Keep together and deliberately work out your position and your best way down.
10 Leave word behind you of your route and when you expect to be back. If you arrive where friends do not expect you, 'phone them or tell the police (to save needless searches).

COUNTRY CODE

1   Guard against all risk of fire.
2   Fasten all gates.
3   Keep dogs under proper control.
4   Leave no litter.
5   Keep to the paths across farmland.
6   Avoid damaging fences, hedges and walls.
7   Safeguard water supplies.
8   Protect wild life, wild plants and trees.
9   Go carefully on country roads.
10 Respect the life of the countryside.

ABBREVIATIONS

AACU	Anti-Aircraft Co-operation Unit
ADG	Air Depot Group
AFS	Advanced Flying School
AFTS	Advanced Flying Training School
AGS	Air Gunners School
AN&BS	Air Navigation & Bombing School
ANS	Air Navigation School
AONS	Air Observers' Navigation School
AOS	Air Observer School
APC	Armament Practice Camp
ATA	Air Transport Auxiliary
ATFERO	Atlantic Ferry Organisation
ATG	Air Transport Group
BATF	Beam Approach Training Flight
BG	Bomb Group
BGS	Bombing & Gunnery School
BS	Bomb Squadron
BTU	Bombing Trials Unit
CANS	Civil Air Navigation School
CCCS	Coastal Command Communications Squadron
CPF	Coastal Patrol Flight
EANS	Empire Air Navigation School
EFTS	Elementary Flying Training School
E&RFTS	Elementary & Reserve Flying Training School
FAA	Fleet Air Arm
FF	Ferry Flight
FG	Fighter Group
FIS	Flying Instructors' School
FLR	First Line Reserve
FPP	Ferry Pilots' Pool
FS	Fighter Squadron
FTG	Fighter Training Group
FTS	Flying Training School
FTU	Ferry Training Unit
FU	Ferry Unit
FW	Fighter Wing
FYS	Ferrying Squadron
HCU	(Heavy) Conversion Unit
HQSFP	Headquarters Service Ferry Pool
IAC	Irish Air Corps
ITS	Initial Training School
KG	Kampfgruppe
MCCF	Maintenance Command Communications Flight
MSFU	Merchant Ship Fighter Unit
MU	Maintenance Unit
OADF	Overseas Aircraft Delivery Flight
OADU	Overseas Aircraft Delivery Unit
OAFU	(Observers) Advanced Flying Unit
OAPU	Overseas Aircraft Preparation Unit
OCU	Operational Conversion Unit
OTU	Operational Training Unit
PAFU	(Pilots) Advanced Flying Unit
RCAF	Royal Canadian Air Force
RCN	Royal Canadian Navy
RFS	Reserve Flying School
RRE	Royal Radar Establishment
RS	Radio School
RU(A)	Repair Unit (Advanced)
SAC	School of Army Co-operation
SAN	School of Air Navigation
SFTS	Service Flying Training School
SGR	School of General Reconnaissance
SPTU	Staff Pilots' Training Unit
TCG	Troop Carrier Group
TCU	(Transport) Conversion Unit
TEU	Tactical Exercise Unit
TFPP	Training Ferry Pilots' Pool
TFW	Tactical Fighter Wing
TRS	Tactical Reconnaissance Sqn
TRW	Tactical Reconnaissance Wing
TTCF	Technical Training Command Communications Flight
TTU	Torpedo Training Unit
TWU	Tactical Weapons Unit
USAAF	United States Army Air Force
USN	United States Navy

BIBLIOGRAPHY

Aircraft Down, Air Crashes in Wharfedale and Nidderdale, B Lunn,Hardwick Publications 1986 and 1988.

The Air War over Gwynedd, Snowdonia Aviation Historical Group

Dark Peak Wrecks, Ron Collier and Ron Wilkinson, 1979

Circular Walks to Peak District Aircraft Wrecks, John D Mason, 1996

Dark Peak Wrecks 2, Ron Collier and Ron Wilkinson, 1980

Fallen Eagles, Edward Doylerush, Midland Counties, 1990

The Last Flight of 43-30719, (C-47 MacGillicuddy's Reeks), Frank Donaldson, Warplane Research Group of Ireland, 1984

The Legend of Landwrog, Edward Doylerush, Midland Counties, 1994

A Moorlands Dedication, (North Staffordshire wrecks), Marshall S Boyland, William H Beech Ltd, 1992

No Landing Place, Edward Doylerush, Midland Counties, 1985

Two Star Red, Gwen Moffatt 1964

Warplane Wrecks of South Wales and the Marches, Peter Durhamand Dewi Jones

Where the Hills Meet the Sky, Peter Clark, Glen Graphics, 1995

Whensoever: 50 Years of the RAF Mountain Rescue Service 1943-1993, Frank Card, 1993

Wings of War Over Gwynedd, Roy Sloan, Gwasg Carreg Gwalch, 1991

Other useful material:

Action Stations, Potted histories of Britain's military airfields and an index. Each volume covers a separate geographical area and the series is essential for providing background information to many of the high ground crashes.

The Lakeland Peaks, The Peak and Pennines, The Scottish Peaks, The Welsh Peaks, W A Poucher, Constable Limited. Full of magnificent photographs and detailed routes. Useful advice on mountain walking and essential equipment.

Wainwright's Lake District Guides, too numerous to list here, are strongly recommended.

We hope that you have enjoyed this Midland Publishing book.
Our titles are carefully edited and designed for you by a knowledgeable and enthusiastic team of specialists, with over 20 years of experience. Further titles are in the course of preparation but we would welcome ideas on what you would like to see. If you have a manuscript or project that requires publishing, we should be happy to consider it; brief details initially, please.

In addition, our associate company, Midland Counties Publications, offer an exceptionally wide range of aviation and railway books/videos for sale by mail-order around the world. For a copy of the appropriate catalogue, please write, telephone or fax to:
Midland Counties Publications, Unit 3 Maizefield, Hinckley Fields, Hinckley, Leics, LE10 1YF. Tel: 01455 233747; Fax: 01455 233737. E-mail: midlandbooks@compuserve.com

BRITISH AIRFIELD BUILDINGS OF WWII

Aviation Pocket Guide 1

Graham Buchan Innes

The world of airfield buildings is one of constant fascination to enthusiasts. Until now, references on this subject have been the domain of very specialist works, or to be partially found within high price books. All of this has conspired to put off a whole army of people who have a thirst for such knowledge.

British Airfield Buildings is the answer to this need and in a genuinely pocket-size form. From control towers, to hangars, to defensive strongpoints, barrack blocks, maintenance buildings to the humble latrine, it provides an illustration of a *surviving* example, highlighting details and other styles of similar building.

Over 200 illustrations with brief but informative captions take the reader for an excursion through a typical wartime station.

British Airfield Buildings provides an ideal primer to a subject close to the heart of all enthusiasts.

Softback
148 x 105 mm, 128 pages
230 b/w photographs
1 85780 026 5
£5.95

AERONAUTICAL PUBS & INNS OF BRITAIN
Aviation Pocket Guide 3

Dave Smith with Ken Ellis

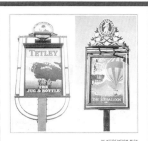

There can be few more perfect combinations than aircraft and pubs. Aviation enthusiasts all over the UK have a passion for both. An amazing number of public houses and inns have strong aeronautical connections.

The *Air Balloon* at Birdlip was a venue for Edwardian ballooning adventures; the *Sir Frank Whittle* in Lutterworth is close to where the first British jet engine ran; the *Bader Arms* was opened by the famous Battle of Britain fighter pilot; and the *Double O Two* near Bristol celebrates the first British-built Concorde.

There is a great fascination in these inns, their signs and their significance, but this book also takes the interest into a much overlooked area – watering holes. All major bomber and fighter stations had favourite places for their airmen to go and unwind.

Topping off a fascinating study is a look at the growing number of aircraft to be found adorning night clubs! A gazetteer of existing aeronautical pubs and inns completes this absorbing guide.

Softback
148 x 105 mm, 96 pages
92 b/w, 3 colour photos, 5 cartoons
1 85780 048 6
£5.95

DISCOVER AVIATION TRAILS
Aviation Pocket Guide 4

Paul Shaw

Interest in aviation museums, airfields used and disused, memorials and other aeronautical venues has never been higher. Enthusiasts are keen to know what to look for and how. Until now, their plans to tour the country relied very much on their own researches – with the risk of missing many 'gems'.

Now an answer is to hand in the popular Aviation Pocket Guide format, a pocket sized collection of twelve regional tours that can be undertaken by car in a day, or over a weekend with 'add ons'. The suggested tours span the country, offering enthusiasts a 'local' to investigate and a many possibilities to be taken up on holiday: Cornwall; Derbyshire/Leicestershire/ Notts; Essex; Lincoln; Lincolnshire; London; Manchester and Cheshire; Norfolk; Northamptonshire; Southern Scotland; South Wales; Yorkshire.

With each tour come plenty of suggestions, each carefully put together to allow for a 'gentle' pace. An ideal travelling companion for enthusiasts of all ages.

Softback
148 x 105 mm, 128 pages
97 b/w, 3 colour photos, 12 maps
1 85780 049 4
£5.95

FlyPast

B ritain's top-selling aviation monthly has a very special place in the hearts of enthusiasts all over the world. Through the years, readers have come to regard *FlyPast* as the magazine covering the world of aviation history, especially its coverage of *living* history. *FlyPast* has never contented itself with just monitoring news of aircraft and events worldwide as they happen, its editorial staff and a network of renowned contributors have built up a reputation as news and opinion makers in their own right. All of this combines to make *FlyPast* the journal that *leads* in the fascinating world of aviation history, museums, displays, operators and aircraft. Don't stand on the touchlines, *take part* with *FlyPast*!

..FlyPast the journal that leads in the fascinating world of aviation history...

In addition, as a subscriber you'll become an automatic member of the *FlyPast* club. This exclusive club was launched to offer its members

fantastic benefits. There's a regular newsletter, special privileges, club discounts on selected items, museum visits, lectures and much, much more.

To ensure you never miss an issue of *FlyPast* place a regular order with your newsagent or take out a post-free postal subscription. See the current issue of *FlyPast* for rates or contact:-
Subscription Dept., Key Publishing Ltd., PO Box 100, Stamford, Lincs., PE9 1XQ. Tel:- 01780 755131, Fax:- 01780 757261 or EMail:- subs@keymags.demon.co.uk.

Full of Facts, Full of Memories